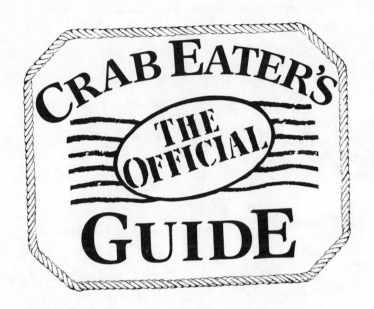

CRAB EATER'S THE OFFICIAL GUIDE

WHITEY
SCHMIDT

MARIAN HARTNETT PRESS

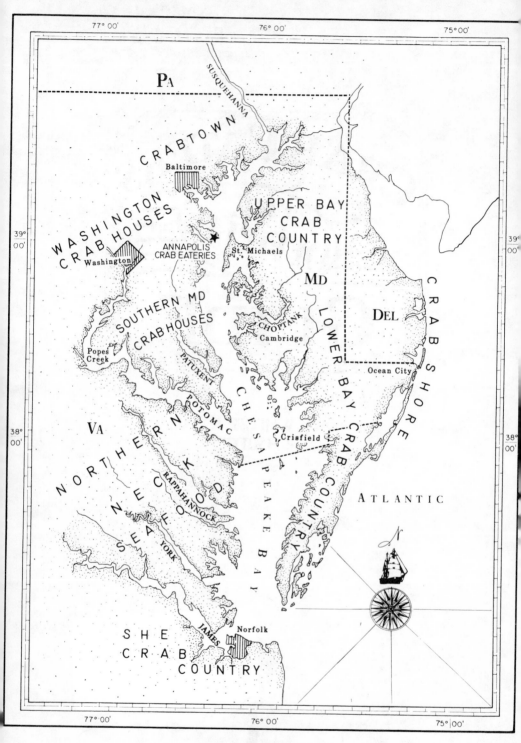

CHESAPEAKE BAY
CRAB REGIONS

II

A
CRAB EATER'S GUIDE
TO THE
CHESAPEAKE BAY
AREA

dedicated to

POP SCHMIDT
&
THE MIDWAY TAVERN

Printed in the
United States of America
First Printing 1985
ISBN 0-9613008-4-1

Library of Congress Catalog Number 83-082989
Copyright © 1984 by Marian Hartnett Press
Box #1417 Suite E20 Alexandria, Virginia 22313

CONTENTS

CONTENTS

FEATURES

Introduction

   This book is written for those people who love hard steamed crabs or for those who simply want to try them for the first time. The Official Crab Eater's Guide will take you to the crab houses and seafood markets that specialize in the art of steaming hard shell crabs and are known for their special touch or recipe. Novice or veteran alike will benefit from The Official Crab Eater's Guide. The listed crab houses and markets are your key to hard shell crabs. Each region is introduced with an easy-to-follow map and listing for that area.

   Our format lists the business season, hours of operation, if the service is eat-in or carry-out and if dockage is available. Crab cookery gives a brief description of some of the delectable crab dishes available.

   The Chesapeake Bay, famed the world over for its bounty, is our geographic setting. Our guide takes the reader through the regions surrounding the Chesapeake Bay. The Bay is a place of extraordinary beauty, extending for almost 200 miles and having a tidewater shoreline of some 4,600 miles. The Bay is dotted with islands and is contributed to by 150 rivers and creeks. It is an endless maze of marshy inlets and hidden coves. Crabbing for the blue crab is a major part of the Bay's heritage and, next to catching them, eating the blue crab is the Bay's favorite pleasure and pastime.

These recommendations and evaluations are entirely our own and were gathered without solicitation or commercial sponsorship. The Official Crab Eater's Guide has personally visited and checked information about each and every establishment listed. However, should there be errors of fact, we apologize and promise, upon notification, to correct them in the next edition.

Naturally, prices and hours of operation are subject to change and, in following the somewhat elusive crab, there are times when individual crab houses may suffer a shortage of supplies. Therefore, it is a good idea to plan ahead and inquire by telephone to place your special crab order. That way you can be assured that it will be hot and steaming when you arrive.

No. 1 Jimmies

Mr. Crab's Sombrero and Crustacean Station;
These names turned up with some investigation.

The Crab Corner, the Crab Cove and Parker's Crab Shore,
Crabs on Wheels, Grab a Crab and Crabs Galore.

Crab King, Imperial Crab and Original Crack Pot,
A-1 Crab Haven, Crab Claw and Crab Pot.

Wicker's Crab, Sleepy Crab, King Crab and Crab Alley,
Happy Crab, Dancing Crab, Crab Shack and Crab Sally.

Olde Obrycki's Crab House and Crab Take-Away,
Marshall's Crab Truck; visit these one day.

The Salty Oyster, The Steamer and the Backfin,
The Cracked Claw, Mug and Mallet and Dinner Bell Inn.

Rod 'N' Reel, House of Crabs, Bob Evan's Bayfood,
Crabbers' Cove, Ms. Lizzie's, Kool Ice and Seafood.

The Crab Bag, Ocean Crab and Crab Cafe,
Crab Net, Crab Line, Crabtowne, U.S.A.

Channel Crab, Country Crab and Crossroads Crab House,
If you're gonna eat crab, of course, take your spouse!

Yesterday's, Today's Catch, Abner's Seaside,
The Poseidon, Seafood Shack, Sea King and Sea Pride.

Barefoot Green's, Brownies, Brown's and The Red Roost,
Capt. White's, Blue Seas and Blue Ridge Seafood.

Riverside, Willoughby's and Windsor are inns,
But Millrace, Kaufmann's and Duffy's, all taverns.

Old Quarterdeck, Sea Hut and House of Neptune,
Old Shuckers, Stop at Bill's and Goodluck Seafood.

Captain Earl's, Cap'n Jim's, Captain Kidd's & Capt. Dick's,
Captain Harvey's, Captain John's, are all good picks.

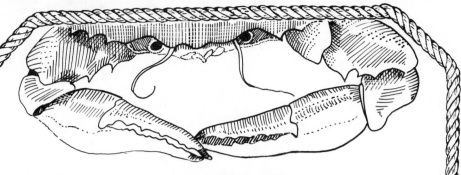

Hubbard's Pier, Port City and Ocean Pride,
Happy Harbor, Harbor Place and The Ebb Tide.

Did you know these places have crabs and more?
Big Apple Market, Crisfield Elks 1044.

There's Bomba's Pizza and Chicken House,
Mr. Bill's, Bo Brook's and Spanky's Club House.

Drift Inn, Howard Hotel and Mick's Quail Inn;
If I eat at all of these, I'll never be thin.

There are places with initials to spend your days;
There's B & G, G & G, JC's and Mr. K's.

P.G.N. Crabhouse and S. Di Paula and Sons,
K. D. Gross, J. A. Jacobs and J. M. Clayton's.

Landmark Crab House is a clue to these names,
Like Shoreline, Pier 7 and Bottom of the Bay.

The Lighthouse, Cain's Wharf, Jug Bridge & Pier Street,
Phillips Waterside, Hemphill's Dock, & Town Creek.

Tom and Terry's, Mike and Jim's and Whitey and Dot's;
This list of names is longer than I thought.

Monaghans, Faidley's, Deitrich's and Marino's,
McNasby's, Pearson's, Price's and Paolino's.

Copsey's, Keyser's, McCoy's and Fenwick's,
Griffin's, Gunning's, Gordon's and Kemp's.

Bob's, Pop's, Todd's and John's,
Gena's, Susan's, Jackie's and Don's.

Melvin's and Mike's and Ted's and Steve's,
Phillips and Sam's and Ross' and Cleve's.

CJ's, Augie's, Roy's and J.C.'s,
These all add up to No. 1 Jimmies.

Lynne Haas

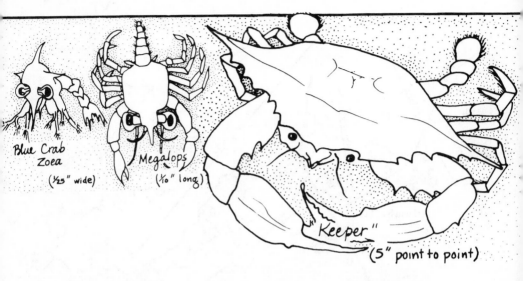

Blue Crab
Zoea
(⅟₂₅" wide)

Megalops
(⅟₁₀" long)

"Keeper"
(5" point to point)

Life of the Blue Crab

Blue Crabs are found in abundance along the Eastern Seaboard but prefer waters which range from ocean saltiness to fresh, thus the Chesapeake Bay provides ideal conditions. Life begins in the Lower Bay where female or "sponge" crabs deposit their eggs between the first of June and the end of August. The baby crabs . . . appear very unlike the mature crab and look more like a swimming question mark . . . This "Zoea" sheds its shell several times, when it begins to resemble the adult, and is then called a "megalops." Typically, crabs hatch from the egg in late June, pass through the larvae stage by August, and start to move up the Bay during early fall, or until the cold weather halts their migration. In the spring their journey is resumed and full maturity is reached when the crab is 12 to 14 months old. In order to increase its size, the crab must molt or shed its outer skeleton. As it approaches a molt it becomes first a "peeler" and as it actually sheds its old shell it becomes a "soft" crab. It is then velvety in texture and roughly ⅓ again as large as the discarded shell. During the struggle for existence, crabs frequently lose legs and claws. Within a week of such loss, a new appendage begins to form, but it takes at least two moltings to fully restore the limb. For some reasons the crab population is very variable and a plentiful season may be followed by a lean one.

Source: The Lighthouse Restaurant Placemat, Virginia Beach, Va.

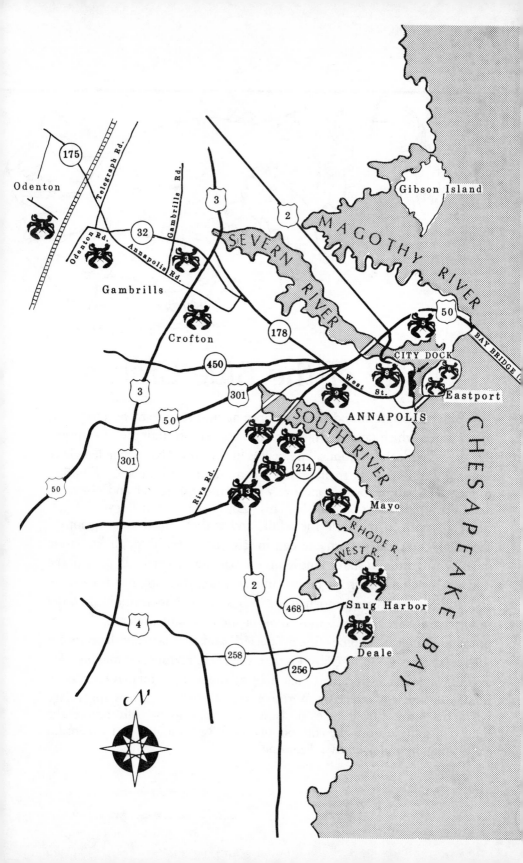

Annapolis Crab Eateries

1. Jim's Hideaway
2. Kemp's Crab Shack
3. Kaufmann's Tavern
4. Shoreline Seafood
5. Riverside Inn
6. McNasby's
7. O'Leary's Seafood Market
8. Annapolis Fish Market
9. Captain Earl's Crab House
10. Pier 7
11. Hayman's Crab House
12. Mike's Bar and Crab House
13. Crab Corner 1
14. Bob Evan's Bayfood
15. K.D. Gross Seafood
16. Happy Harbor Inn

JIM'S HIDEAWAY
1439 Odenton Road
Odenton, Maryland
301/674-2876

Business Season: year round

Hours: Sunday through Thursday—9 AM to 12 midnight,
Friday and Saturday—9 AM to 2 AM

Eat In/Carry Out

Crab Cookery: steamed crabs and homemade crab cakes

Whether you're a connoisseur of crabs and oysters, or if you simply wish to try them for the first time, you owe it to yourself to visit Jim's Hideaway. Located in the tiny town of Odenton, Maryland which is found between Baltimore, Annapolis and Washington, Jim's Hideaway is a well-known and popular spot for business luncheons and family outings.

Since opening in August of 1977, owner Jim Keeney has tastefully added to the already quaint decor by building a screened back porch. It is a comfortable room, used all year round, where Jim serves up crab feasts in the summer season and oyster roasts in the winter. If you prefer, a smaller front room offers patrons the luxury of being served in the ambiance of a room lit by antique lanterns and outside light filtered through stained glass windows. In this atmosphere, Jim serves a delectable fare that will please the palate. Crab feasts include "all the crabs and corn-on-the-cob you can eat—always fresh."

Jim's Hideaway offers a Sunday special from 3:00 to 6:00 featuring steamed crabs, king crab legs, unlimited soup, and includes a salad and hot vegetable bar. To get to Jim's once you are in Odenton, take Route 175 to Morgan Road (adjacent to the Bank of Glen Burnie), continue 1/4 mile to Odenton Road, turn right and you will find Jim's located on the left side of the road.

KEMP'S CRAB SHACK

Odenton and Telegraph Roads
Odenton, Maryland
301/674-2419

Business Season: all year

Hours: Sunday and Monday—10 AM to 6 PM; Tuesday,
Wednesday and Thursday—10 AM to 9 PM; Friday and
Saturday—10 AM to 10 PM

Carry Out Only

Crab Cookery: steamed crabs and crab cakes

Andrew Kemp is your host at this clapboard carry out. He occupies the
space behind the barber shop next to the western wear shop in downtown
Odenton. At Kemp's, "We cater crab feasts and fish fries—soul food."

KAUFMANN'S TAVERN

329 Gambrills Road
Gambrills, Maryland
301/923-2005

Business Season: all year

Hours: 11 AM to 11 PM

Eat In/Carry Out

Crab Cookery: steamed crabs by the dozen or bushel, caters
crab feasts, crab soup, crab salad, crab cakes, and Baltimore
Spice

It is with great pride that the Kaufmann brothers, Dave and Bill,
operate this roadside restaurant. The tavern was a single room built by their
grandfather in 1937. The family continues to operate and renovate; they
now have a 240 seat crab house and are still growing. The live steam cooking
method and the Old Bay Seasoning are the rhyme and reasoning for the
Kaufmann brother's delightfully steamed crabs. My visit recalls delicious
hot steamed crabs and ice-cold Heinekens. This is an airy, rambling and
rambunctious place with a long friendly bar and fast, efficient service. There
is a garden, tended by the family, adjacent to the tavern, which enables the
customers to eat fresh, home grown vegetables with their crabs.

SHORELINE SEAFOOD

1053 Route 3 North
Gambrills, Maryland
301/721-7767

Business Season: all year

Hours: 11 AM to 8 PM, 7 days a week

Carry Out Only

Crab Cookery: steamed hard crabs, soft crabs, and crab meat

Shoreline Seafood is a roadside seafood market catering crab feasts anywhere along the Baltimore-Washington corridor. Owner, Don Storm, seasons with J. O. Seasoning exclusively and prepares crabs with a unique and distinctive taste that will light up your crab-eating palate.

RIVERSIDE INN

Forest Beach Road
St. Margarets, Maryland
301/757-9888 • 301/757-1467

Business Season: mid-April to December

Hours: 7 days a week from 10 AM to 2 AM

Eat In/Carry Out

Dockage Available: Mill Creek

Crab Cookery: Chesapeake steamed crabs, soft crabs, crab soup, and crab cakes

Jimmy Cantler's Riverside Inn is a superb seafood eating experience well worth the drive into suburban Annapolis. This eatery is near the Bay Bridge and you will need directions. Take Route 50 east to Old Mill Bottom Road and turn right. Take the next right onto St. Margarets Road. Go 2 miles, then make a U-turn around Sandy's Store. Make a right turn on Forest Beach Road. Continue to the end. If it sounds like a treasure hunt—it is—with a chest of steamed crabs better than pirate's gold.

Many of the Riverside's visitors arrive by boat as can be seen by the sailboats that line its dock. Also on the dock, is Jimmy Cantler's shedding operation. Here you can see crabs, swimming in shallow floats, that are about to shed their hard shell and become prized soft shells.

McNASBY'S

723 Second Street
Annapolis, Maryland
301/263-3843 • 301/263-3892

Business Season: April 1st to November 30th

Hours: 8 AM to 7 PM daily

Carry Out Only

Dockage Available: Back Creek

Crab Cookery: Maryland steamed crabs and oysters

The best way to enjoy McNasby's Back Creek location is to take the time to walk the streets, feel the spirit of this quaint area, and breathe the fresh salty air. Annapolis is the sailing capital of the east coast. The vast number of sailboats to see is spectacular.

McNasby's—an oyster packing plant in the winter and a crab picking place in the summer, has been offering "Quality Seafood Since 1876" and has, during those 108 years, developed a reputation for quality and good taste.

McNasby's, which specializes in Maryland crabs with J. O. Seasoning, is a special favorite for the crab connoisseur, catering to individuals and to those planning large crab feasts.

O'LEARY'S SEAFOOD MARKET

310 3rd Street
Annapolis, Maryland
301/263-4087

Business Season: open daily

Hours: weekdays—10 AM to 8 PM, weekends—8 AM to 8 PM

Carry Out Only

Dockage Available: Spa Creek

Crab Cookery: soft shell crabs, crab meat, live crabs, and steamed crabs

Tradition, quality, and expertise are important ingredients in any business. Tom O'Leary, new owner of O'Leary's Seafood Market (formerly Sadler's Wharf) knows this and has continued the tradition of excellence that the Sadler family began over 50 years ago. Today, the market carries a variety of new seafood specialties including fresh hand-picked crab meat supplied daily.

ANNAPOLIS FISH MARKET

The Market House, City Dock
Annapolis, Maryland
301/269-0490
301/269-0807

Business Season: summer only

Hours: Monday, Wednesday, Thursday, Friday and Saturday—
9 AM to 6 PM; Sunday—10 AM to 6 PM

Carry Out Only

Dockage Available: Head of the Harbor-Spa Creek

Crab Cookery: live hard and soft crabs, crab cakes on crackers,
and crab soup

The Annapolis Market House, at the city dock, traces its beginnings to
the late 1700's when Annapolis was a bustling colonial seaport. The
modernized market opened in 1972, housing nine retail food businesses and
offering a unique raw bar featuring many delectable crab dishes.

On a cold winter day or a lazy summer afternoon, nothing beats
driving to Annapolis to enjoy the market's endless variety of seafood. Oyster
stew or hot clam chowder may never seem better. And there is crab tasting—
the soup, so delicious, mmm, and the crab cakes are excellent as usual, not
to mention the stand-up raw bar with freshly shucked oysters. You can enjoy
your selection at the stand-up counter looking out of the large windows that
offer a view of the harbor activity on Spa Creek as watermen bring in the
day's catch of crabs, oysters, and fish.

The Naval Academy is within walking distance of the city dock and
makes the market house a must to visit. Enjoy some traditional Maryland
cookery as well as a walk along winding, narrow streets with quaint shops
and the sights and sounds of a busy seaport city.

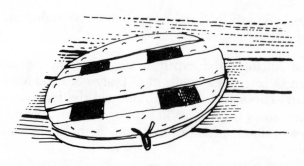

CAPTAIN EARL'S CRAB HOUSE

2023 West Street
Annapolis, Maryland
301/266-8395

Business Season: March through November

Hours: noon to 9 PM—7 days

Carry Out Only

Crab Cookery: J. O. Seasoning, crab cakes to cook at home, soft crabs, and caters to crab feasts

Conveniently located in the heart of the Annapolis business district, Captain Earl's crab cookery is prepared fresh daily. Take home a bag of fresh hot steamed crabs today—you won't be disappointed.

PIER 7

48 South River Road
Edgewater, Maryland
301/956-4422

Business Season: open year round

Hours: 7 days a week from 11 AM to 2 AM

Eat In/Carry Out

Dockage Available: South River

Crab Cookery: Steamed hard crabs, soft crabs, and crab cakes

Pier 7 is located at the foot of the new South River bridge. Here you can enjoy taste-tempting steamed crabs on a patio that looks out to the river. The busy South River offers adventure for sailors in the Annapolis area and Pier 7 is a favorite marina stop. Whether you come by boat or car, you may enjoy a volley ball game on the lawn or you can plan to visit with one of the name bands that perform nightly.

HAYMAN'S CRAB HOUSE

3105 Solomon's Island Road
Edgewater, Maryland
301/956-5656
301/956-2023

Business Season: year round

Hours: 9 AM to 10 PM

Eat In/Carry Out

Crab Cookery: soft crab, imperial crab, crab meat salad, crab soup, and steamed crabs

"Home of the Jumbo," Hayman's Crab House began in 1971 when Roland and Fanny bought a four room bungalow and made it into an eatery. With the help of their son and daughter and many long hours of hard work, they produced a completely remodeled, full-service carry out and restaurant.

Mrs. Hayman thoughtfully includes one of her favorite recipes.

Mrs. Hayman's Crab Soup

2 5 lb. packages of frozen vegetables

3 lbs. potatoes, diced

1 stalk celery, diced

2 #10 can tomatoes

2 large spoons of Old Bay Seasoning

3 lbs. crab meat

2 large spoons of Hayman's Seafood Seasoning and little hot red pepper

Add all ingredients, except crab, to about 2 gals. of water. After boiling hours, add crab meat.

MIKE'S BAR AND CRAB HOUSE
Riva Road
Riva, Maryland
301/956-2784

Business Season: April through October

Hours: Monday through Thursday—11 AM to midnight, Friday through Sunday—11 AM to 1:30 AM

Eat In/Carry Out

Dockage Available: South River

Crab Cookery: Live crabs, steamed crabs, and soft crabs

Many things have changed since 1960 when Mike Piera opened his small bar and crab house, then called the Town Hall. Mike's Bar and Crab House now features a large banquet room with a seating capacity of 300. Not only is it a crab house and bar, but also a general store and marina. With a beautiful view overlooking the South River, Mike's provides good food and a pleasant atmosphere for small or large parties.

Mike shares his method of preparing fried hard crabs:

Fried Hard Crab

Take a cooked hard crab, remove top shell and clean. Place a homemade crab cake on top. Dip in a batter of flour and water made thick. Deep fry for 10 minutes or until golden brown.

11

CRAB CORNER 1
Route 214 and Pike Ridge Road
Edgewater, Maryland
301/798-1107
301/798-0486

Business Season: April to the first week of November

Hours: Tuesday through Friday—3 PM to 7 PM; Saturday, Sunday, and holidays—11 AM to 7 PM

Live Crabs Only

Crab Cookery: live hard and soft crabs, dozens or bushels

Lou Capuano catches, culls, and delivers crabs straight from the water to the roadside, for "fresh" is his trademark. Up at dawn everyday, Lou is a typical Chesapeake Bay waterman, specializing in catching and selling live hard and soft shell crabs.

Lou has developed a unique system to utilize the space and conditions of his Rhode riverside home. It allows him to hold over 3,000 live crabs in his crab pens. With facilities such as this, Lou offers fresh soft shells right off of his truck or hard shells just out of the water. You will appreciate the freshness and may want to visit the Crab Corner 1 often.

BOB EVAN'S BAYFOOD
Central Avenue, Route 214
Mayo, Maryland
301/798-6555

Business Season: April 1st to Christmas

Hours: 11 AM to 8 PM, closed Monday

Carry Out Only

Crab Cookery: crab meat—live, hard, and soft crabs

Bob Evan's Bayfood is an open-air market located in the parking lot alongside of the Mayo Food Center in Mayo, Maryland. Bob and Alexandra are known as the "quality crab people," and their market supplies the commercial crabber with pots, bait, and lines and supplies the crab lover with crabs, seasoning, and salt.

K. D. GROSS SEAFOOD
1478 Gross Circle
and Snug Harbor Road
Shadyside, Maryland
301/867-0802

Business Season: when the crabs are running

Hours: 6:30 AM to dark

Carry Out Only

Crab Cookery: steamed hard crabs and soft crabs, deviled crabs, crab cakes

A drive that pleases, enjoying summer's breezes. . . service so personal and crabs so delicious. . . you'll return again and again. You can count on Kendal Gross to open his carry out sometime in April and, like Ethel, his famous mother, to cook with genuine care fine and tasty crabs.

HAPPY HARBOR INN
Rockhold Creek Drive
Deale, Maryland
301/867-0949 • 301/261-5297

Business Season: all year

Hours: 5 AM to 2 AM , 7 days

Eat In/Carry Out

Dockage Available: Rockhold Creek

Crab Cookery: cream of crab soup, crab cakes and steamed crabs

The Happy Harbor Inn is hosted by Captain and First Mate, Bumpy and Dottie Stowers. They feature weekly specials that are real crowd pleasers. They serve crabs only one day a week—a day to look forward to—and they serve other crab delicacies daily. The Tiki bar is always filled with bayside visitors because of good crabs, great drinks, and a fun-loving atmosphere. Crab soup and corn-on-the-cob are featured in the all-you-can-eat crab feast on Wednesday nights.

From a nautical view, the Happy Harbor Inn is perched just a notch above the new Rockhold Creek bridge and offers what is perhaps one of the best views around these parts. Here, you can view the workboats, the sport crabbers, and power and sailboat enthusiasts, all combining to offer a blend of some of the Bay's finest traditions.

Try the house special, "Little Lester's Captain's Catch."

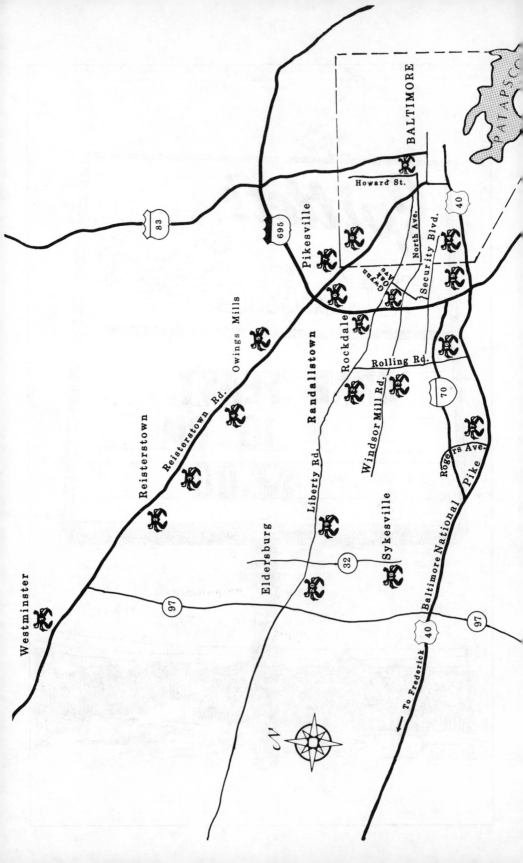

Crabtown

NORTHWEST BALTIMORE

1. Stop At Bill's
2. Blue Sea's Crab House
3. Captain Harvey's Seafood Market
4. Mel's Crab House
5. CJ's Restaurant
6. Backfin Restaurant
7. Gordon's of Pikesville
8. Mr. K's Steamed Crab House
9. The Pump Room
10. Monaghan's Pub
11. Sea King, Inc.
12. Tangier Crab and Oyster House
13. Windsor Inn
14. Millrace Tavern
15. Sea King, Inc.
16. Spittel's Half Shell
17. Spittel's National Pike Crab House
18. Bill's Crab House
19. Tangier Crab House
20. Spanky's Club House

STOP AT BILL'S
2 Washington Road
Westminster, Maryland
301/848-2161

Business Season: all year

Hours: Monday through Friday—9 AM to 6 PM, Saturday and Sunday—9 AM to 9 PM

Carry Out Only

Crab Cookery: live crabs, steamed crabs, and soft crabs

Bernice and Bill Blum's place can be found on the corner of Main and Old Washington Road. When you are in Westminster, Stop at Bill's outstanding carry out for steamed hard shell crabs and fresh produce in season.

BLUE SEAS CRAB HOUSE
11810 Reisterstown Road
Reisterstown, Maryland
301/833-FISH

Business Season: all year

Hours: 11 AM to 9 PM daily

Carry Out Only

Crab Cookery: crab cakes, steamed crabs, soft crabs, live crabs, and fried hard crabs

Blue Sea's Crab House serves restaurant quality seafood at carry out prices. Inquire about bushel sales and crab feast catering of live or steamed crabs.

Bobby's day begins long before most
He's up in the morning and searching the coast
His baited pots are filled with the days good luck
And he brings them home to be sold from his truck.

CAPTAIN HARVEY'S SEAFOOD MARKET

11510 Reisterstown Road
Owings Mills, Maryland
301/356-6688

Business Season: all year

Hours: Monday through Thursday—10 AM to 8 PM,
Saturday—10 AM to 10 PM, Sunday—10 AM to 8 PM

Eat In/Carry Out

Crab Cookery: hot steamed crabs, crab meat, soft crabs, and
imperial crab

In building his all new market, Captain Harvey Marshall expanded to
include seafood treats from around the world. All of his crab delicacies are
packed for travel and can be purchased live or steamed for your trip home.
The Marshall family has served fresh crabs for over 35 years. Inquire about
the Cambridge Room which is open during June, July, and August, where
you will be served delicious crabs prepared with uncommon skill.

MEL'S CRAB HOUSE

1014 Reisterstown Road
Owings Mills, Maryland
301/363-4060

Business Season: all year

Hours: Sunday through Thursday—10 AM to 10 PM, Friday
and Saturday—10 AM to 2 PM

Carry Out Only

Crab Cookery: live and steamed crabs, all lump and special
crab meat

"Mel's 'Space Crabs'—have a taste that's out of this world!"

CJ'S RESTAURANT

10117 Reisterstown Road
at Painter's Mill Road
Owings Mills, Maryland
301/363-6694

Business Season: all year

Hours: Monday through Thursday—11 AM to midnight,
Friday—11 AM to 1 AM, Saturday—3 PM to 1 AM,
Sunday—3 PM to 10 PM

Eat In/Carry Out

Crab Cookery: steamed Maryland and Louisiana crabs

Charlie and Jeanne Sanders opened CJ's in 1978 and since then have
been "serving Maryland seafood in the manner in which it was meant to be
enjoyed. Delicious!" CJ's serves soup and complete dinners. It is "more
than just a crabhouse."

BACKFIN RESTAURANT

1116 Reisterstwn Road
Pikesville, Maryland
301/484-7344

Business Season: all year

Hours: Monday through Thursday—11 AM to 11 PM, Friday
and Satruday—11 AM to midnight, Sunday—2 PM to 11 PM

Eat In/Carry Out

Crab Cookery: hot steamed crabs, crab cakes, and Maryland
crab soup

The Backfin has crabs flown in daily from Louisiana. Owners Charles
Albaugh and Ben Groff "suggest you call ahead to reserve the big ones."

20

GORDON'S OF PIKESVILLE

1017 Reisterstown Road
Pikesville, Maryland
301/484-8343
Carry out: 301/484-2472

Business Season: all year

Hours: 11 AM to 1 AM

Eat In/Carry Out

Crab Cookery: crab soup, steamed crabs, and crab cakes

Located just 1 mile south of Beltway Exit 20, is world renowned Gordon's of Pikesville. Gordon's is rated among the nation's best crab houses and is remembered for having won first prize in a national crab cake contest. Gordon's has been featured in the Time-Life Cookbook Series and is especially noted for its crab soup and garlic crab recipes. The same hot steamed crabs that made Gordon's famous world wide are featured every day, year round.

Althea's Crab Meat Cakes

16 oz. cooked crab meat

½ t. salt

¼ t. black pepper

2 t. onion juice

2 t. parsley flakes

2 eggs beaten

2 t. dry mustard

2 slices dry wheat bread made into crumbs

1 T. baking powder

4 T. oleo or butter softened slightly

¼ t. seafood seasoning

Combine all ingredients and shape into cakes. Pan fry in butter or oleo until browned on both sides. Serves 4.

MR. K'S STEAMED CRAB HOUSE

6309 Reisterstown Road
Baltimore, Maryland
301/764-3900

Business Season: early February to Christmas

Hours: Sunday through Thursday—2 PM to midnight, Friday
and Saturday—2 PM to 1 AM

Eat In/Carry Out

Crab Cookery: steamed crabs, crab soup, and caters crab feasts

Here are subs, sandwiches, and platters to go—or you can enjoy Mr.
K's hard shell crabs freshly steamed to order—mmm.

Helen And John's Crab Cakes

1 lb. backfin crab meat
2 day-old hamburger buns
1 T. parsley
almost ½ C. mayonnaise
a "shake" red pepper
corn flake crumbs
1 T. Old Bay Seasoning
¼ t. salt
1 T. Worcestershire sauce
2 T. water
1 T. finely chopped onion

Go through crab meat to eliminate any shells. Rub hamburger rolls
through hands until very fine and mix with crab meat.

Mix together all other ingredients and add with crab meat.

Divide mixed crab meat into 8 separate piles on wax paper. Shape into
cakes, then coat with corn flake crumbs.

Fry in oil until brown on both sides. Drain on paper towels.
(Alternative: Place crab cakes in shells and bake at 350 degrees for 45
minutes.)

These crab cakes are much better when eaten a day after they are
mixed; this allows the seasonings to penetrate properly.

THE PUMP ROOM
North Avenue and Howard Street
Baltimore, Maryland
301/727-0369

Business Season: all year

Hours: 5 PM to 12 midnight daily

Eat In/Carry Out

Crab Cookery: hot, steamed Louisiana crabs

    The Pump Room has crabs flown in daily from Louisiana. You can be assured of the large ones here. Please call for reservations.
    Patrons of the Pump Room claim that "after 12, the crab turns into a pumpkin."

MONAGHAN'S PUB
2121 Gwynn Oak Avenue
Woodlawn, Maryland
301/944-3311

Business Season: all year

Hours: 11 AM to 11 PM

Eat In/Carry Out

Crab Cookery: hot steamed crabs

    Stop to quench your thirst at the new Monaghan's pub. The bar and lounge serve spicy steamed crabs, tasty with your brew.

SEA KING, INC.
8209 Liberty Road
Rockdale, Maryland
301/655-0110

Business Season: all year

Hours: Monday through Saturday—9 AM to 11 PM, Sunday—9 AM to 10 PM

Carry Out Only

Crab Cookery: cocktail claws, claw crab meat, deluxe crab meat, lump crab meat, soft shell crabs, and hot steamed crabs

Rockdale's Sea King presents the finest in prepared, cooked, or raw seafoods for your enjoyment and convenience throughout the year. One of several Sea Kings, this carry out is located 1 mile northwest of Beltway Exit 18 across from Cook's Department Store.

TANGIER CRAB AND OYSTER HOUSE
9329 Liberty Road
Randallstown Maryland
301/521-2828

Business Season: all year

Hours: Monday through Thursday—10 AM to 11 PM, Friday—10 AM to 12 PM, Saturday—9 AM to 12 PM, Sunday—11 AM to 10 PM

Carry Out Only

Crab Cookery: steamed and live crabs sold by the dozen or bushel, crab meat—claw, special, and backfin, backfin crab cake, deluxe crab cake, regular crab cake, backfin crab fluff, fried hard crab, soft crab fluff, and crab soup

Andy, Bill, and Ed Parks have been serving patrons since 1960. They offer a wide array of specialties that will cater to any crab palate.

"Is your group, club, or organization planning a Crab Feast? Let us know, we'll help your event become a big success with the best in Seafood at Affordable Prices."

WINDSOR INN
7207 Windsor Mill Road
Baltimore, Maryland
301/944-0446

Business Season: all year

Hours: open daily at 11 AM

Eat In/Carry Out

Crab Cookery: hot steamed crabs, crab cakes, and crab soup

The Windsor Inn not only serves Maryland and Louisiana crabs, but offers an ambiance with its fare. Enjoy a crab feast which includes a dozen scrumptious hard shell crabs, a tasty ear of fresh picked Maryland corn, and a bowl of delicious homemade crab soup.

Linda's Crab Sandwiches

1 pound crab meat
1 tablespoon chopped sweet pickle
1 tablespoon chopped onion
1 tablespoon chopped celery
3 tablespoons mayonnaise
½ teaspoon salt
Dash Worcestershire Sauce
2 eggs, beaten
½ cup milk
¼ teaspoon salt
12 slices white bread

Remove any shell or cartilage from crab meat. Combine pickle, onion, celery, mayonnaise, seasonings, and crab meat. Combine egg, milk and salt. Dip one side of each slice of bread in egg mixture. Place bread in a heavy frying pan which contains about 1/8 inch of fat, hot but not smoking. Fry at moderate heat until brown on one side. Drain on absorbent paper. Spread plain side of 6 slices of bread with crab mixture; cover with remaining 6 slices of bread. Place on a well-greased cookie sheet, 15½ x 12 inches. Heat in a moderate oven, 350° F., for 5 to 8 minutes or until heated through.

MILLRACE TAVERN
5201 Franklintown Road
Baltimore, Maryland
301/448-1070

Business Season: all year

Hours: 8 AM to 2 AM daily

Eat In/Carry Out

Crab Cookery: crab imperial (all lump meat), crab cakes, backfin crab fluff, backfin crab cake, soft crab, stuffed fried hard crab, stuffed fried soft crab, hot steamed crabs, and homemade crab soup

This eatery offers a challenge. Will you make it as good as they do?

Millrace Seafood Newburg

6 lbs lobster (cut in pieces)	6 lbs. crab meat
2½ lbs. oleo	6 lbs. scallops
2 gal. hot milk	2 lbs. flour
4 tsp. white pepper	2 oz. salt
7 oz. pimiento and mushrooms (cut pimiento in fine strips)	6 C. sherry wine

Cook raw seafood in 1 lb. oleo. Sauté 1½ lbs. oleo (melted), mix in flour, heat milk and seasoning, add to seafood, add flour and melted oleo paste. Stir well. Add mushrooms, pimiento, sherry. Add crab meat last. Simmer about 25 minutes (stir often). Fish and other seafood can be used in place of some of the seafood called for in this recipe. Makes 5 gallons.

SEA KING, INC.

5230 Baltimore National Pike
Route 40 West
Catonsville, Maryland
301/747-5858

Business Season: all year

Hours: Monday through Saturday—9 AM to 11 PM,
Sunday—9AM to 10 PM

Carry Out Only

Crab Cookery: cocktail claws, claw crab meat, deluxe crab meat,
lump crab meat, soft shells, and steamed crabs

Located next to the Charing Cross Shopping Center, Catonsville's Sea
King offers you unsurpassed quality seafoods.
"This is our guarantee to you." Check it out.

Source: Obrycki's menu cover

SPITTEL'S HALF SHELL
115 North Rolling Road
Catonsville, Maryland
301/788-4666

Business Season: all year

Hours: open every day at 11 AM

Eat In/Carry Out

Crab Cookery: hot steamed crabs in 5 sizes, crab soup, fried stuffed hard crab, crab fluff, and imperial crab

Spittel's has added something new in 1984, offering a crab garden where, by night, you'll enjoy moonlit steamed crabs under the stars, a treat you can't pass up. Tell them Whitey sent you and order the house special, "Little Lester's Captain's Catch."

SPITTEL'S NATIONAL PIKE CRAB HOUSE
8543 Baltimore National Pike
Ellicott City, Maryland
301/465-6171
301/461-2836

Business Season: all year

Hours: open every day at 11:30 AM

Eat In/Carry Out

Crab Cookery: hot steamed crabs in 5 sizes, crab soup, fried stuffed hard crab, crab fluff, and imperial crab

Les Spittel opened his first crab house in 1967. He now has restaurants serving seafood in three Baltimore area locations; each eatery is managed by a Spittel family member.

BILL'S CRAB HOUSE

7610 Main Street
Sykesville, Maryland
301/795-5660

Business Season: all year

Hours: Thursday, Friday, and Saturday—4 PM to 10 PM,
Sunday—2 PM to 7 PM

Carry Out Only

Crab Cookery: steamed crabs, soft crabs, crab cakes, crab fluff
and fried hard crabs

Bill Clarius serves hot and delicious crabs in his "down by the
riverside" crab house. Bill's Crab House was the local firehouse for over 50
years. It's a surefire good bet for crab eating.

TANGIER CRAB HOUSE

1945 Liberty Road
Eldersburg, Maryland
301/549-1161

Business Season: all year

Hours: Monday through Thursday—10 AM to 11 PM,
Friday—10 AM to 12 PM, Saturday—9 AM to 12 PM,
Sunday—11 AM to 10 PM

Carry Out Only

Crab Cookery: steamed and live crabs, hard and soft crabs, crab
meat, and fried hard crabs

You may stop in when just passing through or phone ahead for quick
service. Or you can do what we did. While sitting at a table on the outdoor
patio, we opened our bag of crabs-to-go, slowly taking in the aroma of well-
seasoned fresh crab, and then proceeded to polish off one dozen crabs,
lickety-split, cracking those shells.

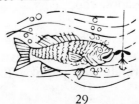

SPANKY'S CLUB HOUSE
1043 Liberty Road
Eldersburg, Maryland
301/795-8444

Business Season: all year

Hours: Tuesday, Wednesday, and Thursday—11 AM to 10 PM;
Friday and Saturday—11 AM to 11 PM; Sunday—11 AM to
9 PM

Eat In/Carry Out

Crab Cookery: hot steamed crabs and crab cakes

Low on price and high on spice, join charter club members Sandy,
Mike, and Jim in the "Our Gang" club house for delicious steamed crabs.
Crab cooking begins after 5 PM on weekdays and all day on Saturday
and Sunday.

Crab Imperial Avocado

1 green pepper, chopped fine

2 strips red pimiento, diced

1 T. dry mustard

1½ t. salt

½ t. pepper

2 raw eggs

1 C. mayonnaise

3 lbs. backfin crab meat

paprika

2 avocados, chopped

Combine all ingredients except crab and blend. Add crab carefully to
keep lumps intact. Heap into crab shells or individual casserole dish. Top
lightly with mayonnaise. Sprinkle with paprika. Bake in oven at 350° for
about 5 minutes.

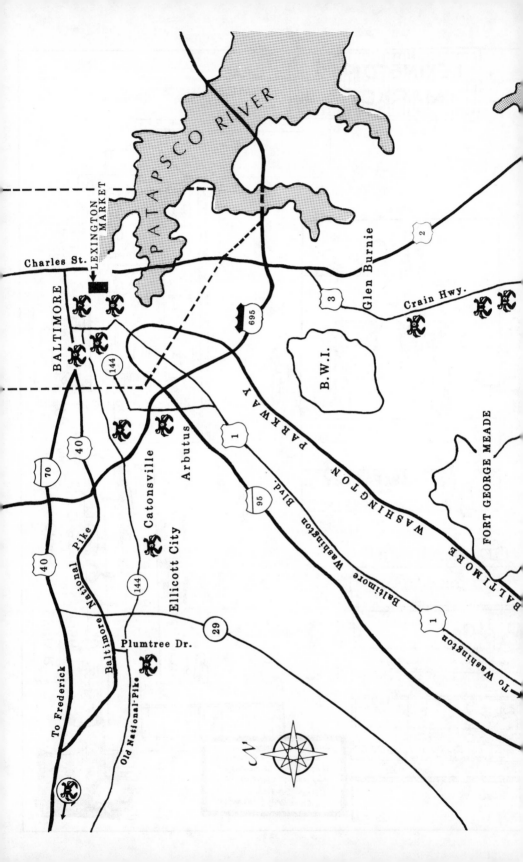

Crabtown

SOUTHWEST BALTIMORE

1. Jug Bridge Seafood
2. The Crab Shanty
3. Sea Hut Inn
4. The Crab Shack
5. Sea Pride Crab House
6. Bay Island Seafood
7. The Crab Pot, Inc.
8. John W. Faidley Seafood
9. Capt. Dick's Crabs Galore!!
10. Dietrich Seafood
11. Crabtowne U.S.A., Inc.
12. Marino's House of Seafood

JUG BRIDGE SEAFOOD

9009 Baltimore National Pike
Frederick, Maryland
301/663-9898 • 301/694-6197
301/694-9895

Business Season: March to January

Hours: Monday through Sunday—11 AM to 11 PM, closed
Tuesday

Eat In/Carry Out

Crab Cookery: hot steamed crabs

Jug Bridge's source for crabs extends from Delaware to Florida,
including Maryland and Virginia, Georgia, Louisiana, Texas, North
Carolina, and South Carolina. Steamed crabs seasoned with a secret blend of
J.O. Seasoning are cooked to order. Jug Bridge's provides pleasant
surroundings for eating crabs that "melt in your mouth." Try their
Thursday all-you-can-eat crab feast.

THE CRAB SHANTY

3410 Plumtree Drive
Ellicott City, Maryland
301/465-9660

Business Season: all year

Hours: Monday through Saturday—9 AM to 11 PM,
Sunday—9 AM to 10 PM

Eat In/Carry Out

Crab Cookery: cocktail claws, claw crab meat, crab meat, soft
shell crabs, and steamed crabs

While passing through the Baltimore area, stop to enjoy the rustic
charm of this country crab house and sample the fresh and tasty crabs
seasoned to delight the palate.

SEA HUT INN

729 Frederick Road
Catonsville, Maryland
301/788-0388

Business Season: all year

Hours: Monday through Thursday—10 AM to 10 PM, Friday
and Saturday—10 AM to 2 AM

Eat In/Carry Out

Crab Cookery: hot steamed crabs, crab cakes, and soft crabs

Don't be misled by the small store front entrance of the Sea Hut—
inside is a complete raw bar and a 5,000 square foot restaurant. "We carry a
full line of fresh seafood and hot spicy crabs." Try 'em.

THE CRAB SHACK

3111 Frederick Road
Baltimore, Maryland
301/566-1600

Business Season: all year

Hours: Thursday through Sunday—11 AM to 10 PM

Carry Out Only

Crab Cookery: hard crabs—live or steamed, by the dozen or
bushel

The Crab Shack's many-pepper seasoning is a taste you won't want to miss.

SEA PRIDE CRAB HOUSE

Pratt and Monroe Streets
Baltimore, Maryland
301/624-3222
301/624-3223

Business Season: all year

Hours: Friday and Saturday—11 AM to 2 AM, Sunday—11 AM to 12 AM, Monday through Thursday—12 PM to 12 AM (winter hours may be shorter)

Carry Out Only

Crab Cookery: hot steamed crabs

Conveniently located in the heart of the Baltimore business district, the Sea Pride's streetside crab house offers crabs from Maryland, Virginia, Georgia, Florida, and North Carolina that are delectably seasoned with J.O. Spice.

BAY ISLAND SEAFOOD

1903 West Pratt Street
Baltimore, Maryland
301/566-0200

Business Season: all year

Hours: 10 AM to 1 AM daily

Carry Out Only

Crab Cookery: steamed crabs, fried crabs, live crabs, crab meat, and crab cakes

"Bay Island crabs can't be beat." This one makes crabs the ultimate treat.

REGISTERED TRADE MARK

"CAN'T BE BEAT"

THE CRAB POT, INC.
Lexington Market
Lexington & Eutaw Streets
Baltimore, Maryland
301/752-7686

Business Season: all year

Hours: 9 AM to 6 PM

Carry Out Only

Crab Cookery: specializing in steamed crabs, crab cakes, and seafood party trays

The Crab Pot is located in the world famous Lexington Market, which has been a thriving marketplace since 1782. While there is a staggering array of food vendors at the market, the Crab Pot stands out. It offers crab cookery with a special flavor that is a real delight for market visitors.

JOHN W. FAIDLEY SEAFOOD
Lexington Market
Lexington and Eutaw Streets
Baltimore, Maryland
301/SARATOGA 74898

Business Season: all year

Hours: 7:30 AM to 6 PM

Eat In/ Carry Out

Crab Cookery: live or steamed crabs, soft crabs, crab meat, backfin crab cakes, crab soup, regular crab cakes on bread or on crackers. and soft crab sandwiches.

J. W. Faidley's is a family tradition dating back to 1887. Located in the world famous Lexington Market, this eating place is a seafood lover's delight. Try hot steamed crabs, freshly shucked oysters and clams, or some of the hot crab delights, quick fried and made ready to be enjoyed at the stand-up counter. You can't sit down at Faidley's, but you won't need to in order to enjoy Maryland's "largest raw bar."

CAPT. DICK'S CRABS GALORE!!

5618 South Western Boulevard
Arbutus, Maryland
301/242-2191

Business Season: all year

Hours: weekdays—4 PM to 10 PM, Friday—2 PM to 11:30 PM, Saturday—11 AM to 11 PM

Carry Out Only

Crab Cookery: live and steamed crabs by the bushel and by the dozen, soft crabs, and crab meat

Put Capt. Dick's on the top of your crab eating list. Capt. Dick knows his crabs and you can bet money that you will be eating some of the finest crab cookery offered in the Washington/Baltimore area. Capt. Dick uses only the freshest crabs and knows best how they should be prepared.

DIETRICH SEAFOOD

440 Crain Highway, N.W.
Glen Burnie, Maryland
301/766-7808

Business Season: year round

Hours: Monday and Wednesday—4 PM to 9 PM, Tuesday – closed, Thursday and Sunday—11 AM to 9 PM, Friday and Saturday—10 AM to 10 PM

Carry Out Only

Crab Cookery: live crabs, hot steamed crabs cooked to order by the dozen or bushel, backfin crab cake, crab fluff, imperial crab, crab soup, and soft crabs

Need catering for your crab feast? Want a good crab cake? Want a crab fluff? Want some good crab soup? Want soft crab fresh from the Maryland shore? You want Dietrich Seafood!

CRABTOWNE U.S.A., INC.
1500 Crain Highway
Glen Burnie, Maryland
301/761-6118

Business Season: all year

Hours: open 24 hours a day

Eat In/Carry Out

Crab Cookery: crab cakes, soft crabs, and hot steamed crabs

Picnic tables, pinball and plenty of crabs prove to be a plus at Crabtowne. See the Crabtowne showcase for their selection of steamed hard shell crabs.

MARINO'S HOUSE OF SEAFOOD
1810 Crain Highway, S.W.
Glen Burnie, Maryland
301/761-7696
For Crabs Only Call:
301/766-1499

Business Season: year round

Hours: Monday through Wednesday—10 AM to 11 PM, Thursday and Friday—10 AM to 12 PM, Saturday—10 AM to 12 PM, Sunday—10 AM to 11 PM

Eat In/Carry Out

Crab Cookery: live or steamed crabs, wholesale and retail, fried hard crabs, large crab cakes with crackers, crab cakes with roll, crab fluff, and crab soup

Words can't describe this kind of eatin'!

According to "Ye Maryland Chronicle" written for the Baltimore Sunday Sun in 1933, the Maryland crab was the main reason for Captain John Smith's visit to the Chesapeake Bay in 1607. Crab cakes were first eaten by Lord Baltimore in 1634. The Imperial Crab was created in honor of Queen Henriette Marie.

Maryland Department of Natural Resources

42

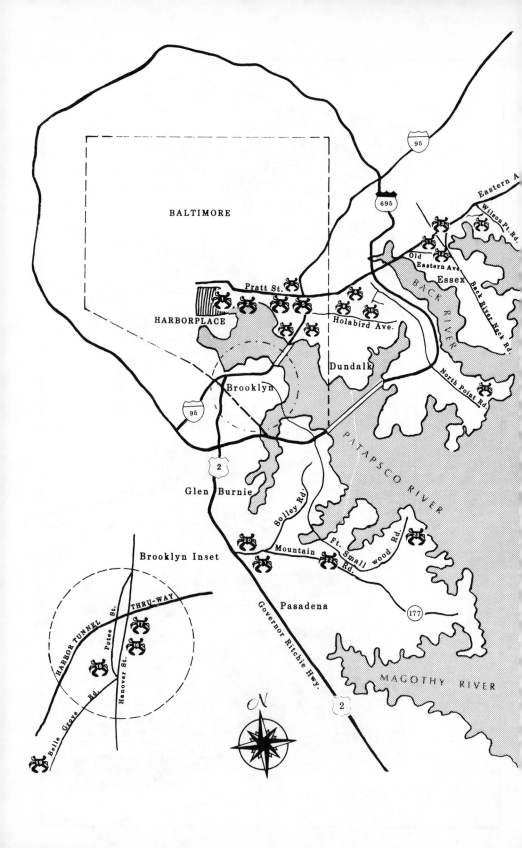

BALTIMORE

95

695

Eastern A.

Wilson Pt. Rd.

Old
Eastern Ave.

Essex

BACK RIVER

Back River Neck Rd.

Pratt St.

HARBORPLACE

Holabird Ave.

North Point Rd.

Dundalk

Brooklyn

PATAPSCO RIVER

95

2

Glen Burnie

Solley Rd.

Ft. Smallwood Rd.

Mountain
Rd.

Brooklyn Inset

THRU-WAY

Pasadena

177

Governor Ritchie Hwy.

HARBOR TUNNEL

Potee St.

Hanover St.

Belle Grove Rd.

MAGOTHY RIVER

2

N

Crabtown

SOUTHEAST BALTIMORE

1. Phillips Harborplace
2. Connolly's Seafood House
3. Al's Seafood
4. John's Carry Out
5. Olde Obrycki's Crab House
6. Chris' Crab House
7. Bud Paolino's Crab & Oyster House
8. Ross' Crab House
9. The Crab Net
10. House of Neptune
11. Al's Seafood Restaurant
12. A-1 Crab Haven
13. Schultz's Crab House
14. Whitey & Dot's
15. Augie's
16. Gunning's Crab House
17. Crab Alley
18. Price's Seafood
19. Crab Cove Restaurant and Lounge
20. Anne Arundel Crab House, Inc.
21. Spittel's Half Shell
22. Chesapeake Bay Seafood
23. Gunning's of Stoney Creek

PHILLIPS HARBORPLACE

301 Light Street
Baltimore, Maryland
301/685-2722
301/547-9060

Business Season: all year

Hours: 11 AM to 11 PM

Eat In/Carry Out

Dockage Available: Inner Harbor

Crab Cookery: steamed crabs, box of crab claws, special crab
meat, claw fingers, backfin lump meat, crab cake, backfin crab
cake, jumbo crab cake, soft shell crab, vegetable and cream of
crab soup, crab imperial, crab salad, crab thermidor, and crab
lumps au gratin

A reputation can sometimes be difficult to live up to. Phillips has never
had that problem. So, when they opened the Baltimore Harborplace
location, there was no doubt that they would be tremendously successful.

As usual, Phillips serves only the freshest crabs, steamed to perfection.
Or, if you prefer, your crab meat can be prepared anyway you wish it to be,
again, to perfection.

In addition to a full service cocktail lounge and restaurant, Phillips
offers a raw and stew bar, carry out, fresh seafood market, and cafeteria
service.

The restaurant is decorated in the traditional Phillips style—Victorian.
Tiffany lamps, stained glass windows, and other period items are as much a
part of the Phillips trademark as their reputation for fine food and prompt,
courteous service.

Harborplace has much to offer its visitors and Phillips will provide a
special highlight.

CONNOLLY'S SEAFOOD HOUSE

Pier No. 5
705 Pratt Street
Baltimore, Maryland
301/727-9551
301/727-9268

Business Season: year round (crabs—April to November, oysters—November to April)

Hours: Monday through Thursday—10 AM to 11 PM, Friday and Saturday—10 AM to midnight, Sunday—11 AM to 10 PM

Dockage Available: Inner Harbor

Eat In/Carry Out

Crab Cookery: crabs (any style) in season

Connolly's restaurant is part of a family tradition dating back over 67 years and is one of the few waterfront establishments to survive recent renovations. Connolly's unique eating place has an air of nostalgia created by old ice cream parlor chairs around the tables, a pleasant contrast to the hustle and bustle of an active and picturesque waterfront.

AL'S SEAFOOD

Fleet and Wolfe Streets
Fells Point
Baltimore, Maryland
301/327-2646

Business Season: all year

Hours: Sunday through Thursday—11 AM to 11 PM, Friday
and Saturday—11 AM to midnight

Carry Out Only

Crab Cookery: steamed crabs, soft crabs, crab cakes, crab fluff,
and catered crab feasts

Fells Point, which dates back to 1730, is Baltimore's most significant
portside neighborhood. It is the home of a variety of marine activities
including delicious carry out crab dishes from Al's Seafood.

JOHN'S CARRY OUT

3001 O'Donnell Street
(corner of Potomac Street)
Baltimore, Maryland
301/276-7222

Business Season: May to Thanksgiving

Hours: 9 AM to 11 PM

Carry Out Only

Crab Cookery: backfin crab cake, crab soup, crab fluff, soft
crab, fried hard crab, and live or steamed crabs

Do you like fresh dough pizza, fresh Greek salad, or a delicious crab
cake sandwich, then try John's Carry Out. "We take the time to cook your
order to satisfaction."

OLDE OBRYCKI'S CRAB HOUSE

1729 East Pratt Street
Baltimore, Maryland
301/732-6399

Business Season: April through October

Hours: Tuesday through Saturday—11 AM to 10 PM

Eat In/Carry Out

Crab Cookery: the best crabs all summer

The Olde Obrycki's menu tells the story:

"Olde Obrycki's Crab House is located in two restored townhouses on land that was part of the original William Fell estate, in the area now known as historic Fells Point. The corner building at 1729 East Pratt Street was built in 1851, and the adjoining building at 1731 was built the following year.

The magnificent old oak bar, with its thirteen mirrors depicting the thirteen original colonies, was constructed in place in 1865, the year Abraham Lincoln was assassinated. A gentleman by the name of Charly Wedig opened a tavern there that year, and it is very possible that soldiers quartered at the Union Camp of the 7th Maine Regiment at Patterson Park stopped in for a beer at the end of a long day. From 1866 until Prohibition in 1920, there were several different tavern owners, the most notable being George Gunther of the Gunther Brewing Company.

In 1944, Melvin Alexander purchased the property, and together with his brothers-in-law, Mitch, Joe and Eddie Obrycki, ran a bar operation. Eventually, they decided to expand their business by serving food, featuring the delectable Maryland blue crab. At that point, Obrycki's became a restaurant.

When Melvin, Mitch and Joe relocated and started a separate business of their own in 1949, Eddie and his wife, Eleanor took over what became known as Ed Obrycki's Olde Crab House. This partnership continued until 1976, when they sold the restaurant to Richard and Rose Cernak, who, together with their four children, are carrying on the Obrycki tradition."

CHRIS' CRAB HOUSE
801-805 South Montford Avenue
Baltimore, Maryland
301/675-0117

Business Season: all year

Hours: open 6 days a week (closed Mondays)—11 AM to 10 PM

Carry Out Only

Crab Cookery: live and steamed crabs, crab meat and soft crabs—"We cater crab feasts."

Chris' Crab House is a popular Baltimore neighborhood crab carry out conveniently located on the corner of Montford Avenue and Fait Avenue. It is now in its 23rd year of business.

BUD PAOLINO'S CRAB & OYSTER HOUSE
3919 East Lombard Street
Baltimore, Maryland
301/732-4080

Business Season: year round

Hours: open every day from 8 AM to 2 AM

Eat In/Carry Out

Crab Cookery: hot steamed Bay, Texas, and Louisiana crabs, crab cakes, crab soup, and crab fluff

Nationally famous, "Buds" opened in 1945 serving, not crabs, but meatball sandwiches. Today, his specialty is crabs and 335 crab lovers can be seated in the enclosed beer garden. You will enjoy the expansion of the bar and the live entertainment, not to mention the delicious crab dishes.

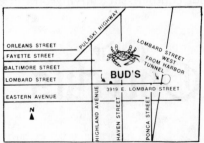

ROSS' CRAB HOUSE

1109 Old North Point Road
Dundalk, Maryland
301/288-1200

Business Season: all year

Hours: 9:30 AM to 11 PM, 7 days

Carry Out Only

Crab Cookery: homemade crab soup, live crabs, soft crabs, crab meat, crab seasoning, crab mallets, crab fluff, fried hard crab stuffed, crab cakes, and hot steamed crabs

Dick and Helen Ross have divided their crab house into three departments in order to serve you better. They say, "Our #1 department is crabs...Since crabs are our business, we try to make sure we have crabs all year. We have floats built in southern waters to assure us of our supply in the winter when good crabs are hard to get. These crabs are not dredged; they are sandfree...Crabs are steamed with our own seasoning, blended by Baltimore Spice and made up of 33 spices; it originated in 1961."

THE CRAB NET

7703 German Hill Road
Baltimore, Maryland
301/282-6266

Business Season: crabs year round

Hours: closed Monday, Tuesday—11 AM to 11:30 PM, Wednesday and Thursday—11 AM to 12:30 AM, Friday and Saturday—11 AM to 1:30 AM, Sunday—1 PM to 11:30 PM

Eat In/Carry Out

Crab Cookery: live or steamed hard crabs and crab meat

This family seafood restaurant offers cold beer, best in the summer, a warm fireplace in the winter, and hot and fat crabs spirited with seasoning.

HOUSE OF NEPTUNE

7600 Holabird Avenue
Baltimore, Maryland
301/284-6820

Business Season: all year

Hours: 9 AM to midnight

Carry Out Only

Crab Cookery: hot and heavy, steamed, and live crabs

"For Maryland's best, try Neptune's crabs." The King of the Sea has to have the best catch.

AL'S SEAFOOD RESTAURANT

1515 Eastern Boulevard
at Stemmers Run Road
Essex, Maryland
301/687-3264

Business Season: all year

Hours: Sunday through Thursday—11 AM to 11 PM, Friday and Saturday—11 AM to midnight

Eat In/Carry Out

Crab Cookery: steamed crabs, live crabs, and crab meat

Al's Seafood is a complete seafood market that caters crab feasts and oyster roasts and is a popular roadside restaurant with a tremendous local following. At Al's, "The crabs you eat tonight flew Eastern today."

A-1 CRAB HAVEN

1600 Old Eastern Avenue
Essex, Maryland
301/687-6000

Business Season: all year

Hours: Monday through Thursday—11 AM to midnight, Friday and Saturday—11 AM to 1 AM, Sunday—11 AM to 11 PM

Eat In/Carry Out

Crab Cookery: hot steamed crabs and crab cakes

Be sure to check out the clown collection in the bar and look for the Annual Pot Luck Sale, long famous as the main attraction for Blue Channel Crabs. Their dining room is one of the most beautiful in the state.

SCHULTZ'S CRAB HOUSE

1732 Old Eastern Avenue
Essex, Maryland
301/687-1020

Business Season: year round

Hours: 10 AM to 2 AM, 7 days

Eat In/Carry Out

Crab Cookery: crab fluff, backfin crab cake, crab soup, fried hard crab, and hot spicy steamed crabs

Bob McKinney opened his Baltimore crab house in 1968 and has since created a colorful atmosphere in which you will enjoy the eating of crabs. Large windows, knotty pine panels, blue tables and walls, ceiling fans, and plenty of photographs taken by Bob, add to a pleasant atmosphere.

WHITEY & DOT'S
1110 Beech Drive
Baltimore, Maryland
301/686-9720

Business Season: April to November

Hours: Monday through Friday—10 AM to 2 AM, Sunday—10 AM to 9 AM

Eat In/Carry Out

Dockage Available: Darkhead Creek on Middle River

Crab Cookery: hard crabs and crab cakes

Eat crabs while overlooking the Middle River in this traditional waterman's bar. Whitey and Dot's crab house was opened in 1949 and the family tradition continues today, offering large crabs to be eaten in front of a large fireplace, a heart-warming, palate-pleasing, winter treat.

AUGIE'S
Millers Island Road
Millers Island, Maryland
301/477-1305

Business Season: April through November

Hours: 11 AM to 9 PM

Carry Out Only

Crab Cookery: "For the Finest of Steamed Crabs"

Augie's is a superb seafood experience well worth a drive. No matter what part of the Bay you are on you may want to go there, for the fare is simple: good hard shell crabs.

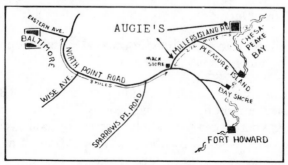

GUNNING'S CRAB HOUSE

3901 South Hanover Street
Brooklyn, Maryland
301/354-0085

Business Season: all year

Hours: Monday through Thursday—11 AM to midnight;
Friday, Saturday, and Sunday—11 AM to 2 AM

Eat In/Carry Out

Crab Cookery: crab soup, soft crab fluff, imperial crab,
crabman's platter, backfin crab cake, and steamed crabs

Crabs are available year round from Louisiana, Texas, and the
Chesapeake Bay, the land of pleasant living. Ed Gunnings, who has been
serving since 1969, features crabs steamed "the old fashioned way" using a
steel pot, ½ inch of water, salt and spice to taste—simple and delicious.
In 1969, Gunning's was a corner bar with an enclosed garden in the
back. In order to bring in more business, Ed steamed three bushels of crabs.
This was the beginning of a thriving trade that has expanded to what used to
be an auto sales lot next door. This lot is now a beer garden and the auto
sales office has been transformed into Gunning's carry out. Crab lovers will
love it! From three bushels of crabs came a garden that can accommodate
300 crab eaters.

CRAB ALLEY

3733-35 South Hanover Street
Brooklyn, Maryland
301/354-1190

Business Season: all year

Hours: 10 AM to 2 AM, 7 days

Eat In/Carry Out

Crab Cookery: hot steamed crabs, soft crab sandwich,
fried hard crab, crab fluff, crab soup and imperial crab

In a friendly, neighborhood atmosphere, Crab Alley offers some of the
best crab eating in Baltimore. Here you will find tasty and colossal crabs,
conscientious service and a special ambiance.

PRICE'S SEAFOOD

Corner of Potee and Talbot Streets
Brooklyn, Maryland
301/355-4725

Business Season: all year

Hours: Monday through Friday—12 PM to 10 PM, Saturday—
12 PM to 11 PM, Sunday—10 AM to 11 PM

Carry Out Only

Crab Cookery: live crabs, steamed crabs (by the dozen or by
the bushel), caters to crab feasts, soft crab sandwiches, crab cake
sandwiches, fried hard crab, crab cake fluff, soft crab fluff, crab
soup, and frozen or live soft shell crabs

In the family for 20 years, Price's Seafood serves a complete catalog of
crab delicacies. Many claim this is the best crab stop in "Crabtown." We
will let you be the judge.

CRAB COVE RESTAURANT AND LOUNGE

5622 Belle Grove Road
Brooklyn, Maryland
301/789-6761

Business Season: all year

Hours: 11 AM to 1 AM

Eat In/Carry Out

Crab Cookery: hot steamed crabs, crab soup, crab cakes, and
soft crabs

Mr. John and Mr. Ray say: "Our crabs make our customers happy!"
The evidence is the smiling faces of patrons who are eating golden crab cakes
with large chunks of lump crab meat fresh from the Maryland shore and
mixed with the Crab Cove's own special ingredients. You will smile too
when you try the soft shell crabs, pan fried to a golden crisp, sweet
and delicious.

ANNE ARUNDEL CRAB HOUSE, INC.

Mountain and Solley Road
Pasadena, Maryland
301/255-3344

Business Season: all year

Hours: Tuesday and Wednesday—9 AM to 8 PM, Thursday through Saturday—9 AM to 10 PM, Sunday—10 AM to 8 PM

Eat In/Carry Out

Crab Cookery: steamed crabs, live crabs, soft crabs, crab cakes, and crab cake fluff

The colorful Anne Arundel Crab House sits on the corner of Mountain and Solley Road. The building that once housed a service station is now a seafood market complete with a crab picking plant. You can be sure this crab meat is fresh.

SPITTEL'S HALF SHELL

Ritchie Highway and Mountain Road
Glen Burnie, Maryland
301/766-5266

Business Season: all year

Hours: open every day at 11:30 AM

Eat In/Carry Out

Crab Cookery: crab soup, fried stuffed hard crab, crab fluff, imperial crab, and hot steamed crabs

Open for lunch and open for dinner, this Spittel's location is surely a winner. All of the delicious crab dishes are readily made available for carry out. If you prefer you can enjoy your selection in the spacious restaurant or in the Crab Garden.

CHESAPEAKE BAY SEAFOOD

2412 Mountain Road
Pasadena, Maryland
301/255-9880

Business Season: all year

Hours: Monday through Saturday—8 AM to 9 PM, Sunday—
8 AM to 7 PM

Carry Out Only

Crab Cookery: crab cake; soft crab; crab fluff; crab meat—claw,
special, and backfin; and live and steamed crabs

Dorothy Clough is the chief cook, crab steamer, and bottle washer of
this popular seafood market, now in its 30th year of outstanding crab
cookery. Try 'em, you won't be disappointed.

GUNNING'S OF STONEY CREEK

8238 Fort Smallwood Road
Pasadena, Maryland
301/437-2722

Business Season: year round

Hours: 11 AM to 10 PM daily

Eat In/Carry Out

Crab Cookery: backfin crab cake, crab fluff, fried soft crab, and
hot steamed crabs

Located at the foot of the Stoney Creek Bridge, Ed Gunnings is your
gracious host. Stop in and tell him Whitey sent you and enjoy some great
crab eating.

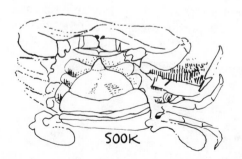

SOOK

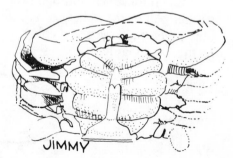

JIMMY

CRAB PICKIN' GET CRACKIN'

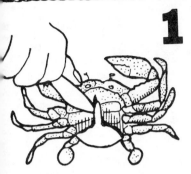

1

With knife, pry off apron flap

2

Lift off top shell.

3

With top shell removed, simply scrape areas A, B, and C. The delectable crab meat lies just under the thin membrane cover.

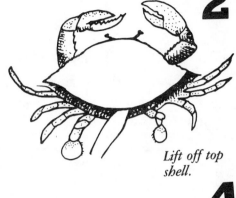

4

Break off claws and swimming legs. The legs have a tasty morsel inside them as well.

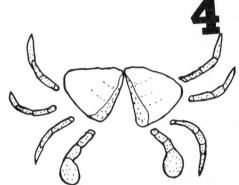

5

Meat under the membrane can be exposed by removing this cover. With knife, slice lengthwise through the center. Each half will reveal large, succulent chunks of meat.

Don't smash 'em, just crack 'em.

"Without you, our dear customers, we would not be. So thank you from Neptune the Legendary Lord of the Sea."

Source: Bo Brook's Menu

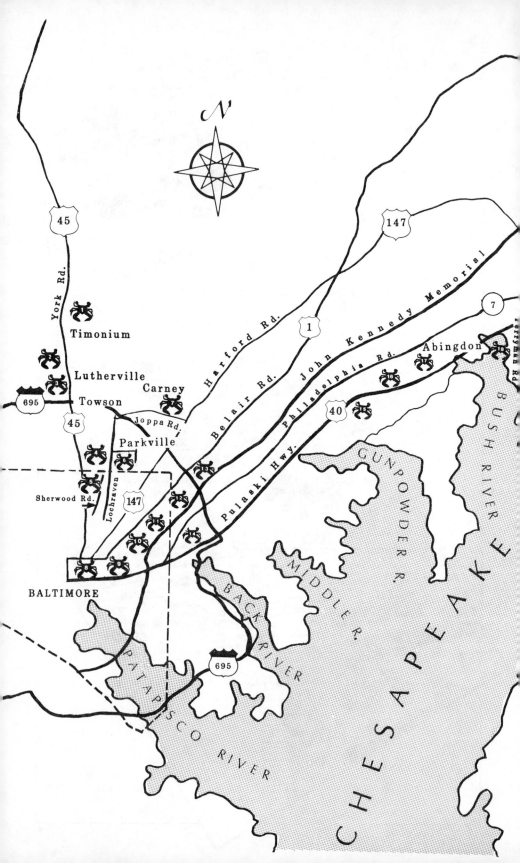

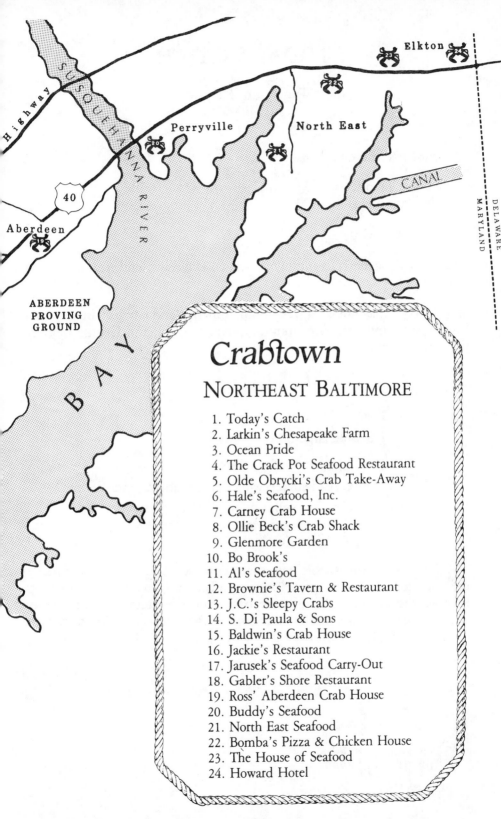

Crabtown

NORTHEAST BALTIMORE

1. Today's Catch
2. Larkin's Chesapeake Farm
3. Ocean Pride
4. The Crack Pot Seafood Restaurant
5. Olde Obrycki's Crab Take-Away
6. Hale's Seafood, Inc.
7. Carney Crab House
8. Ollie Beck's Crab Shack
9. Glenmore Garden
10. Bo Brook's
11. Al's Seafood
12. Brownie's Tavern & Restaurant
13. J.C.'s Sleepy Crabs
14. S. Di Paula & Sons
15. Baldwin's Crab House
16. Jackie's Restaurant
17. Jarusek's Seafood Carry-Out
18. Gabler's Shore Restaurant
19. Ross' Aberdeen Crab House
20. Buddy's Seafood
21. North East Seafood
22. Bomba's Pizza & Chicken House
23. The House of Seafood
24. Howard Hotel

TODAY'S CATCH

2142 York Road
Timonium, Maryland
301/561-0151

Business Season: all year

Hours: Monday through Saturday—10 AM to 6 PM,
Sunday—noon to 5 PM

Carry Out Only

Crab Cookery: crab meat, hard crabs, live crabs, and steamed
crabs

Today's Catch offers a fresh seafood market and raw bar. In a location
just opposite the state fair grounds, Steve, Willard, and George welcome
your crab orders.

Alice's Brown Baggers

1 dozen live crabs

1 double large brown paper bag

Crab mixture:

    Mix 2 C. ketchup with 1 oz. ground cayenne pepper.

    Add 3 t. of crab boil or Old Bay Seasoning.

    Add 1 t. vinegar. Add 2 t. horseradish.

    Add 1½ t. salt.

Put crabs in the double bag; shake down kinda flat. Place on a pan in
the oven for 20 minutes at 150 degrees. This will put the crabs to sleep.
Remove the bag of crabs. Slit the bag down the middle. With a pastry
brush, spread crab mixture all over both sides of the crabs. Return crabs to
oven for 15 minutes with heat at 250 degrees.

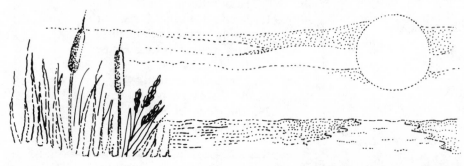

LARKIN'S CHESAPEAKE FARM
1534 York Road
Lutherville, Maryland
301/296-2722

Business Season: all year

Hours: Monday through Wednesday—10 AM to 7 PM, Thursday—10 AM to 8 PM, Friday and Saturday—10 AM to 9 PM, Sunday—1 PM to 7 PM

Carry Out Only

Crab Cookery: crab cakes, imperial crab, steamed crabs, crab meat, crab fluffs, and soft crabs in "the State of Maryland's oldest seafood house"

Capt. Jack Larkin provided us with the following information:

"Since 1867 our tradition. . .is firmly rooted by the founding fathers of Larkin's Seafood, starting with two generations in Europe, then migrating to this country to establish four more generations in the business of handling quality seafood.

Known throughout the nation, the men at Larkin's strive to uphold the policies set forth by their predecessors in the day to day personal attention in which they deal with each customer's orders.

Daily, we are serving Maryland's finest restaurants, clubs, seafood companies and allied food service establishments through 'Larkin's Seafood,' and shipping the nation's finest through our wholly owned subsidiary, 'Chesapeake Farm.'

In 1968, the Chamber of Commerce of Metropolitan Baltimore honored Larkin's Seafood, when they presented us with the coveted 100 years citation, the only seafood company in Maryland so recognized.

The Baltimore News American stated that 'Larkin's earned a reputation for outstanding service and are deserving of their special niche in city history.'

Quality merchandise backed by service. . .our pledge. . . our tradition."

OCEAN PRIDE

1540 York Road
Lutherville, Maryland
301/321-7744

Business Season: all year

Hours: Sunday—9 AM to 10 PM, Monday through Thursday—7 AM to 11 PM, Friday and Saturday—7 AM to 1 AM

Eat In/Carry Out

Crab Cookery: crab feast specialty, crab cake, crab fluff, fried hard crab, soft crab, Maryland crab soup, and hot steamed crabs

Ocean Pride is a relaxed, informal crab house where you can feel at home with prompt, courteous service of excellent steamed crabs in an enclosed beer garden.

THE CRACK POT SEAFOOD RESTAURANT

8102 Loch Raven Boulevard
Baltimore, Maryland
301/828-1095

Business Season: all year

Hours: Friday and Saturday—11 AM to 12 midnight, Sunday through Thursday—11 AM to 11 PM; crabs are served after 5 PM daily

Eat In/Carry Out

Crab Cookery: hot steamed crabs, crab cakes, and crab soup

Louisiana crabs are flown in especially for you every day—sprinkled with the Crack Pot's own special blend of seasoning and rock salt and stacked ceremoniously in front of the crab lover. Bushels of crabs, live or steamed, are available from June to September. "But," says the Crack Pot, "we are not just for crabs."

OLDE OBRYCKI'S CRAB TAKE-AWAY
6318 Sherwood Road
Baltimore, Maryland
301/377-8575

Business Season: April to end of October

Hours: Thursday, Friday, Saturday—4 PM to 9 PM, Sunday—
3 PM to 8 PM

Carry Out Only

Crab Cookery: hot, delicious steamed crabs

Baltimore's long-famous Obrycki's crabs are now readily available at
Olde Obrycki's Crab Take-Away.

HALE'S SEAFOOD, INC.
1801 Taylor Avenue
Parkville, Maryland
301/665-4000

Business Season: all year

Hours: Monday through Saturday—10 AM to 10 PM,
Sunday—10 AM to 9 PM

Carry Out Only

Crab Cookery: live or steamed and hard or soft crabs and crab
meat

Hale's Seafood, Inc. has been a favorite Baltimore carry out for over 20
years. Located on the corner of Taylor Avenue and Oakleigh Road, Hale's
offers live and steamed crabs by the dozen or bushel. "We serve crabs the
year round and specialize in Florida crabs during the winter months. Having
a crab feast? Give us a call."

CARNEY CRAB HOUSE

2014 East Joppa Road
Baltimore, Maryland
301/665-5000

Business Season: year round

Hours: weekdays—9 AM to 2 AM, Friday and Saturday—9 AM to 3 AM

Eat In/Carry Out

Crab Cookery: hot steamed Maryland, Louisiana, and Texas crabs, and caters to crab parties

Carney Crab House is located East of Beltway Exit 30 and requests that you "Let us be your Crab House." Carney's welcomes groups and parties and if you are planning a trip—"we will pack your crabs to go."

OLLIE BECK'S CRAB SHACK

Moravia and Belair Roads
Baltimore, Maryland
301/483-2426

Business Season: open in April, close in November

Hours: Monday through Thursday—4 PM to 11 PM, Friday and Saturday—12 PM to 12 AM, Sunday—2 PM to 11 PM

Carry Out Only

Crab Cookery: Bay crabs only—steamed, live, soft shell crabs, and crab meat

Ollie Beck's Crab Shack is located in the rear of Ollie Beck's Sub Haven.

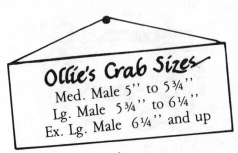

Ollie's Crab Sizes
Med. Male 5" to 5¾"
Lg. Male 5¾" to 6¼"
Ex. Lg. Male 6¼" and up

GLENMORE GARDEN

4813 Belair Road
Baltimore, Maryland
301/488-2366

Business Season: year round

Hours: 9 AM to 2 AM daily

Eat In/Carry Out

Crab Cookery: steamed crabs and crab cakes

Inside Glenmore Garden, you will find an English pub atmosphere with beamed ceilings, dart boards and dark wood. Outside, in the garden, there is room to seat 300 crab lovers. Enjoy the feast on Monday and Thursday from 5 PM to 10 PM.

Judy's Crab Cakes

1 lb. freshly picked crab meat

1 egg

¼ C. finely chopped green pepper

2 T. finely minced onion

1 T. mayonnaise

1 t. Old Bay Seasoning

In bowl, beat egg slightly. Add remaining ingredients and crab meat and mix gently and thoroughly. Shape into cakes.

Melt 2 T. butter in non-stick fry pan. Over medium heat, fry cakes until golden brown on each side.

BO BROOK'S

5415 Belair Road
Baltimore, Maryland
301/488-8144
Carry Out Telephone: 301/488-CRAB

Business Season: year round

Hours: lunch—11 AM to 3 PM, dinner and steamed crabs—5 PM to 1 AM, Sunday—11 AM to 10 PM

Eat In/Carry Out

Crab Cookery: all crab specialties are prepared with Bo Brook's crab meat—imperial crab cake, crab imperial, crab fluff, soft crab platter (close your eyes and let your taste buds savor), stuffed soft crab fluff (stuffed and dipped, delicious and juicy) and hot steamed crabs

The following is taken from Bo Brook's menu:

In the year 1971 Neptune the legendary Lord of the seas was in a calm and generous mood. He stretched out his hand and raised Bo Brooks from one dining room to three. From there he progressed us to four.

Neptune the legendary Lord of the sea.

For you our customers, our Texas Dock, to reap the harvest of the ocean floor. Crustaceans so inviting that he stepped us to five.

Neptune the legendary Lord of the sea.

Our seafood plant upon the land he applied. Lump meat, backfin, claw and fingers cooked and picked. Shipping is required.

Neptune the legendary Lord of the sea.

Five to six he so did order. A cooler building large enough for the treasures. From Maryland to Texas to Mexico shall be our borders.

Neptune the legendary Lord of the sea.

A meeting was called and King Neptune did preside. A larger restaurant was in order for Bo Brooks to reside. Ballots were claw carried from oceans to seas. From one to seven is destined to be. Neptune the legendary Lord of the seas gave his Blessing and crab lovers the address is now.......5415.......

WITHOUT YOU, OUR DEAR CUSTOMERS, WE WOULD NOT BE. SO THANK YOU FROM

Neptune
the Legendary Lord of the Sea

71

AL'S SEAFOOD
6663 Belair Road
Overlea
Baltimore, Maryland
301/426-7878

Business Season: all year

Hours: Sunday through Thursday—11 AM to 11 PM, Friday and Saturday—11 AM to midnight

Eat In/Carry Out

Crab Cookery: fried crab, crab soup, crab cakes, and steamed crabs

Cayenne pepper added to salt and vinegar makes an excellent dip for the succulent backfin chunks that the crab picker first enjoys upon opening the hot steamed crab. The first bite is worthy of the gods. This seasoning awaits you at Al's. Care to join me?

BROWNIE'S TAVERN & RESTAURANT
7703 Belair Road
Baltimore, Maryland
301/661-7538

Business Season: all year

Hours: 7 AM to 2 PM daily

Eat In/Carry Out

Crab Cookery: hot steamed crabs and crab cakes

Brownie's Tavern is located inside Beltway Exit 32 South and boasts, "Our crabs come from Louisiana and Texas."

J. C.'S SLEEPY CRABS
8027 Belair Road
Baltimore, Maryland
301/661-5910

Business Season: February through December

Hours: Monday through Friday—5 PM to 2 AM, Saturday and Sunday—1 PM to 2 AM

Eat In/Carry Out

Crab Cookery: serving Louisiana jumbo crabs

"Paul Newman eats J.C.'s sleepy crabs."

S. DI PAULA & SONS
7613 Philadelphia Road
Baltimore, Maryland
301/866-8100

Business Season: entire year

Hours: open 7:30 AM

Carry Out Only

Crab Cookery: live and frozen soft crabs, and live or steamed hard crabs

S. Di Paula's was established in October of 1897. It serves many of Baltimore's clubs, institutions, hospitals, nursing homes, and restaurants in addition to catering crab feasts for individuals. Live crabs are steamed with a special mixture created by Baltimore Spice Company.

BALDWIN'S CRAB HOUSE
525 Pulaski Highway
Joppa, Maryland
301/679-0957

Business Season: all year

Hours: 2 PM to 11 PM daily

Eat In/Carry Out

Crab Cookery: crab cake, soft crab, crab fluff, fried hard crab, soft crab fluff, and steamed hard shell crabs

Charles Baldwin, your host since 1979, offers: "Our specialty—hot steamed crabs the Maryland way."

JACKIE'S RESTAURANT
3702 Pulaski Highway
Abingdon, Maryland
301/676-9008
301/679-6770

Business Season: year round

Hours: 11 AM to 2 AM

Eat In/Carry Out

Crab Cookery: hot steamed crabs, crab cakes, crab fluff, imperial crabs, and crab soup

Jackie and Tom Keyser specialize in Texas and Louisiana crabs during the winter and local river crabs in the summer. "We believe we cook as good a crab here as anywhere in the country." We think you may agree.

JARUSEK'S SEAFOOD CARRY-OUT
Pulaski Highway
Abingdon, Maryland
301/676-4994

Business Season: May to November

Hours: Tuesday through Thursday—2 PM to 9 PM, Friday and Saturday—11 AM to 9 PM, Sunday—10 AM 'till sold out

Carry Out Only

Crab Cookery: steamed crabs, fresh crab meat, soft crabs, and crab cakes

Jarusek's, "The Crab Place," is located on U.S. Route 40 between Aberdeen and Edgewood. Try it!

GABLER'S SHORE RESTAURANT
2200 Perryman Road
Aberdeen, Maryland
301/272-0626

Business Season: May to 2nd Sunday after Labor Day

Hours: 11 AM, 6 days; closed Mondays

Eat In/Carry Out

Dockage Available: Bush River

Crab Cookery: hot steamed crabs

Gabler's Shore is reminiscent of an early summer camp dining hall. You will eat in an almost beach-like atmosphere with windows that open inward to allow for gentle breezes from the Bush River. You can also enjoy your crabs at picnic tables by the water's edge under the tall trees. You must sample this one.

ROSS' ABERDEEN CRAB HOUSE

625 Route 40
Aberdeen, Maryland
301/575-6813

Business Season: all year

Hours: 9:30 AM to 11 PM daily

Carry Out Only

Crab Cookery: fresh crabs, crab meat, soft crabs, and steamed crabs

Dick and Helen Ross opened their Aberdeen Crab House in 1968 and boast of 2,000,000 crabs sold over a two year period. That's a lot of crabs!

BUDDY'S SEAFOOD

Route 40
Perryville, Maryland
301/642-6456

Business Season: all year

Hours: Monday through Friday—6 AM to 11 PM, Saturday and Sunday—9 AM to 11 PM

Eat In/Carry Out

Crab Cookery: hot crabs, crab meat, crab cakes, and soft shell crabs

Buddy's Seafood is located at Twin Oaks and offers a picnic area. Call ahead for reservations and group parties and watch for specials on Wednesday nights.

NORTH EAST SEAFOOD
195 Main Street
North East, Maryland
301/287-8380

Business Season: April through October

Hours: 10 AM to 7 PM

Carry Out Only

Crab Cookery: hard and soft, live and steamed, and Maryland
and Virginia crabs

North East Seafood cooks crabs the old fashioned way with one inch of
vinegar and water in a steel pot on a gas stove. J.O. #2 crab spice is used with
black pepper to season the crabs and crushed red pepper is added
for zest.

BOMBA'S PIZZA & CHICKEN HOUSE
Route 40
North East, Maryland
301/287-9474

Business Season: year round

Hours: Sunday through Thursday—11 AM to midnight, Friday
and Saturday—11 AM to 1 AM

Eat In/Carry Out

Crab Cookery: steamed crabs and ''Bomba's Crab Cakes''

Jimmy Bomba's crab cakes have long been featured at the Fair Hill
Races, a yearly benefit of the Union Hospital in Elkton, Maryland. Jimmy
now adds steamed crabs to his pizza and chicken fare.

THE HOUSE OF SEAFOOD

222 South Bridge
Elkton, Maryland
301/398-7110

Business Season: all year

Hours: 10 AM to 10 PM

Eat In/Carry Out

Crab Cookery: crabs live or steamed, crab soup, crab claws, and soft shell crabs

The House of Seafood, which is located next to the Elk Mall, is a 300 seat restaurant and seafood market.

HOWARD HOTEL

101 West Main
Elkton, Maryland
301/398-4646

Business Season: March 15th to November 1st

Hours: 10 AM to midnight

Eat In/Carry Out

Crab Cookery: steamed crabs and crab cakes

The Howard Hotel is renovating the upstairs loft and preparing for indoor crab feasts (call for details). This hotel is over 200 years old and offers a charming, natural, all wood decor.

A flyer was handed to me as I entered the Howard Hotel and answered all of my crab feasting questions:

"This is to advise you that we are prepared to supply your needs for steamed crabs this season. We handle all grades and sizes to meet your crab feast needs no matter what price range you choose.

We can deliver warm crabs in the quantity you need. We will also hold as many in back-up as you desire and will take back any crabs you may have left after your feast for only a small service charge."

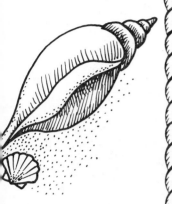

Ode to the CRAB

Sweet meat on spindly legs scurry.
Furtive eyes dart
Hither; thither.

He moves like the waves
Which wash his domain.
He has the moon for a companion,
The seasons for a guide.
He searches for food, a mate,
A safe place to molt, or sleep,
Owning a simple existence.

Yet suspicion and pride
Seem his most marked characteristics,
As if he knows
Even dead, even cooked,
He will not easily
Relinquish himself.

Fitting like a glove
His shell house
And pincher claws
Conjure monster visions
In his tiny brain—
His protection against hungry seekers.

He guards himself
Like a prize, a delight,
A morsel of ambrosial degree.

Legends say he's a present/lesson
Directly from the Creator.
Crab meat lovers learn
The best things come
In small and hard packages—
Sometimes leg by leg.

Lynne Haas

*"The upper Chesapeake Bay region is dotted
with farm land, bayside towns and villages,
and rivers with classic names like Bohemia,
Sassafras, and Chester."*

Source: Maryland Department of Economic
and Community Development

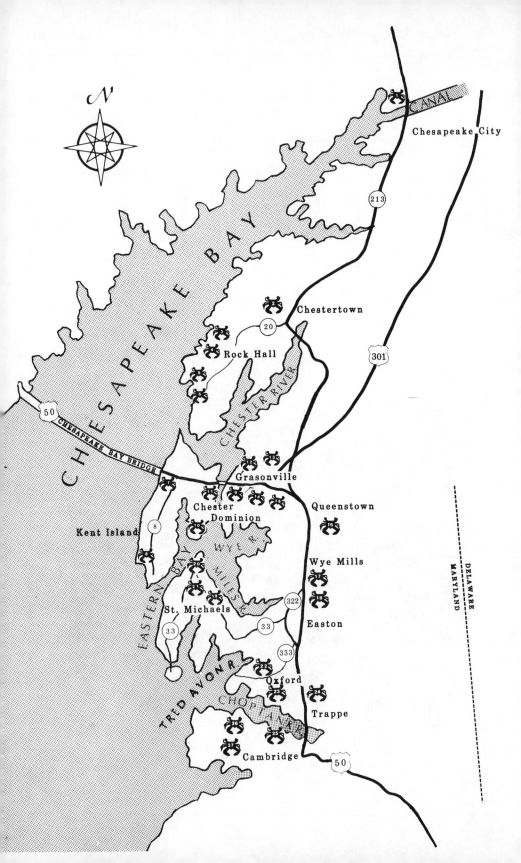

Upper Bay
Crab Country

1. Shirk's Seafood, Inc.
2. Chestertown Seafood
3. Cain's Wharf
4. J. A. Jacobs Seafoods
5. Hubbard's Pier and Seafood, Inc.
6. Rock Hall Seafood
7. Hemingway's Seafood Restaurant
8. Kentmorr Marina
9. Seafood Unlimited
10. George Hill, Jr. & Sons Seafood, Inc.
11. The Ebb Tide
12. Harris' Crab House
13. The Poseidon Restaurant
14. Droter's Anglers Marina
15. Fisherman's Seafood Market, Inc.
16. Capt. Jim's Seafood Kettle
17. Wye River Seafood
18. Cooper's "Crab Shack"
19. The Salty Oyster
20. The Crab Claw
21. Big Al's Seafood Market
22. Town Creek Restaurant and Marina
23. Pier Street Restaurant
24. Pop's Market
25. Kool Ice and Seafood
26. The J. M. Clayton Company
27. Todd Seafoods, Inc.

SHIRK'S SEAFOOD, INC.
Route 213
Chesapeake City, Maryland
301/885-2244

Business Season: March to November

Hours: 10 AM to 6 PM daily

Carry Out Only

Crab Cookery: steamed crabs, live crabs, and crab meat

Crabs, corn and cantaloupe characterize the life style of the colorful people who live and work in the upper Bay crab country. The warmth and friendliness of the people are evident for those who linger long enough to find out. A stop at Shirk's roadside seafood market is a must in order to give one an accurate impression of the upper Bay plus a sample of delicious steamed crabs.

CHESTERTOWN SEAFOOD
206 Cannon Street
Chestertown, Maryland
301/778-5959

Business Season: all year

Hours: 7 AM to 6 PM, closed Sunday

Carry Out Only

Crab Cookery: hard crabs, soft crabs, and crab meat

The upper Chesapeake Bay region is dotted with farm land, bayside towns and villages, and rivers with classic names like Bohemia, Sassafras, and Chester. Another delight of this unique area are crabs steamed by Chestertown Seafood—hot 'n' spicy. This eatery is located at Kibler Coal Yard.

CAIN'S WHARF
Walnut Street
Rock Hall, Maryland
301/639-7379

Business Season: May through October

Hours: 9 AM to 5 PM daily

Carry Out Only

Dockage Available: Rock Hall Harbor

Crab Cookery: live or steamed and hard or soft crabs; caters
crab feasts

Cain's Wharf, located on Walnut Street in Rock Hall, may be a little difficult to find, but your visit is well worth the effort. On first arriving, you get that special feeling that only a waterfront seafood market surrounded by beautiful yachts can give. Once inside, the Cain family hand selects and prepares your crabs to order. The market's pleasant rustic charm and unique cooking method provide the ingredients for a delightful evening of crab cookery.

J.A. JACOBS SEAFOODS
South Hawthorne Ave.
Rockhall, Maryland
301/639-2319

Business Season: May through November

Hours: 9 AM to 8 or 9 PM daily

Carry Out Only

Dockage Available: Rock Hall Harbor

Crab Cookery: Maryland crabs steamed with a special mixture
of J.O. Seasoning

Why are J. A. Jacobs Seafoods so delicious? Crabs steamed with a special mixture made by J.O. Spice are part of the secret; fresh quality products and high pressure steam are others.

HUBBARD'S PIER AND SEAFOOD, INC.
Hawthorne Avenue
Rock Hall, Maryland
301/778-4700

Business Season: June through October

Hours: 8 AM to 6 PM daily

Carry Out Only

Dockage Available: Rock Hall Harbor

Crab Cookery: steamed Maryland crabs

"Home of the striped bass," Hubbard's also steams up great crabs.

ROCK HALL SEAFOOD

Sharp Street Wharf
Rock Hall, Maryland
301/639-2261
301/778-1803

Business Season: all year

Hours: 5 AM to 6:30 or 7 PM daily

Eat In/Carry Out

Dockage Available: Rock Hall Harbor at the mouth of the Chester River and the Chesapeake Bay

Crab Cookery: Maryland crabs seasoned with J.O. Seasoning, crab cakes, and crab imperial

The following is one of Rock Hall's tasty crab recipes:

Rock Hall Crab Imperial

1 lb. crab meat	¼ C. margarine
pinch of salt of pepper	3 T. flour
2 T. worcestershire sauce	bread crumbs
¾ C. milk	3 T. chopped green peppers
mustard	

Mix in bowl crab meat, salt, pepper, green pepper, mustard, worcestershire sauce, and Old Bay. In saucepan, melt butter over low heat, add flour, and stir until smooth. Add milk and cook until thickened to make white sauce. Add crab mixture and stir until heated through and all mixture is covered with sauce. Put in container, cover top with bread crumbs and bake at 400° for 20 minutes.

ROCK
HALL
SEAFOOD

HEMINGWAY'S SEAFOOD RESTAURANT

Pier One Marina
Stevensville, Maryland
301/643-CRAB
301/643-2196

Business Season: May 1st to September 30th

Hours: Thursday and Friday—5 PM to midnight, Saturday and Sunday—1 PM to 12 PM

Eat In/Carry Out

Fly: Bay Bridge Airport

Dockage Available: Pier One Marina and Chesapeake Bay

Crab Cookery: soft crabs or steamed hard Maryland crabs with Baltimore Spice

David and Leslie Harper are your gracious hosts at this completely remodeled bayside crab house. Eat crabs right on the shore of the Chesapeake Bay, inside or outside on the wide front lawn. Try them by car, by boat, by plane. If you are driving, Hemingway's is at the eastern end of the Bay Bridge. At the traffic light by the bridge, turn south onto Route 8 and then take the next right. If you arrive by sea, just pull up to the convenient dock. If you fly into the Bay Bridge Airport adjacent to the marina, Hemingway's authentic English taxi cab will pick you up and deliver you to the restaurant and, after a delicious meal, will return you to the airport.

KENTMORR MARINA

Route 8
Kent Island, Maryland
301/643-4500

Business Season: April to November

Hours: noon to 10 PM

Eat In/Carry Out

Dockage Available: Kent Island **Fly:** Kent Island Air Park #7532

Crab Cookery: 21 herbs and spices make up the house
seasoning created by Baltimore Spice, crab soup, crab cakes,
baked lump imperial crab, and hard crabs are cooked to order

Fly! Motor! Sail! to this "Old Maryland Style Crab House" at
Kentmorr Marina on Kent Island in the heart of pleasant living. Kent Island
centers around a small air park that is within walking distance of the crab
house. If you are driving, it is located five miles south of the Bay Bridge on
Route 8.

We discovered Kentmorr Marina at the end of October. Since this was
the last day of the season, the staff and employees were celebrating their
annual Christmas party. Our order was quickly filled, and we joined in the
festive spirit.

Where else but in the land of pleasant living can you find Christmas
trees, champagne, and colossal crabs. . .in October.

SEAFOOD UNLIMITED

Route 18
Kent Narrows, Maryland
301/827-6525

Business Season: all year

Hours: 8 AM to 8 PM, weekdays. . .later on the weekends

Carry Out Only

Crab Cookery: steamed crabs

The best steamed crabs are those that have been just pulled from the
water and popped into the pot, and while the Seafood Unlimited is a new
listing in our search for the best crabs, we are eager and ready to sample our
next dozen of freshly steamed crabs. Will I see you there?

GEORGE HILL, JR. & SONS SEAFOOD, INC.
Dominion Road
Chester, Maryland
301/643-2121, 2122, or 2506

Business Season: year round

Hours: 8 AM to 6 PM

Carry Out Only

Crab Cookery: live and hot steamed crabs by the dozen or bushel

George Hill, Jr. and sons have designed their crab truck to cater those special occasions when you and your friends will enjoy fresh, hot spiced crabs cooked and served in your own back yard.

THE EBB TIDE
Piney Creek Road
Chester, Maryland
301/643-6053
301/643-5282

Business Season: all year

Hours: 11 AM to 10 PM, 7 days

Eat In/Carry Out

Crab Cookery: steamed hard crabs by the dozen, bushel, or truckload, soft crabs, crab salad, crab soup, crab imperial, and caters crab feasts

There is always a crowd at The Ebb Tide where the food is served on picnic tables and the aroma of steamed crabs and the sound of laughter makes the experience a celebration. The Ebb Tide includes a seafood market on the premises and boasts: "Our crabs are caught and delivered daily by our own watermen."

HARRIS' CRAB HOUSE
Sewards Point Road
Grasonville, Maryland
301/827-8104

Business Season: May through October

Hours: weekdays—4 PM to 11 PM, Saturday and Sunday—11 AM to 11 PM

Eat In/Carry Out

Dockage Available: Kent Narrows

Crab Cookery: "We have live or steamed hard crabs and soft crabs to take home."

"GRAB A CRAB"...welcomes you to the seafood paradise on the straits of Kent Narrows. Dock at the pier and eat inside or out on the sundeck patio. Capt. Bill Harris has made steamed crabs fresh from the Bay his specialty since 1948.

THE POSEIDON RESTAURANT
Route 50 at Kent Narrows
Grasonville, Maryland
301/827-7605

Business Season: May 15th through October

Hours: Thursday, Friday, Saturday, Sunday, and Monday—11 AM to 11 PM

Eat In/Carry Out

Dockage Available: Kent Island, Mears Point

Crab Cookery: steamed hard crabs

The Poseidon Restaurant offers live entertainment and both indoor and outdoor service. The new outdoor crab deck seats 200 crab eaters. We leave the choice up to you—hot steamed crabs outside or elegant inside dining in one of the most picturesque and unique nautical restaurants on the eastern shore.

DROTER'S ANGLERS MARINA
Route 18
Grasonville, Maryland
301/827-6717

Business Season: April to November

Hours: open at 5 AM

Eat In/Carry Out

Dockage Available: Kent Narrows

Crab Cookery: hard and soft Bay crabs, live or steamed

Bert and Cass are your hosts at this bay side restaurant and bar. They offer the crab lover daily bushel sales. Droter's has a great view of the wake and boats from a close perspective. As we sipped some cold brew at our table, we watched the watermen prepare the crabs they had harvested that day for our eating.

☆ ☆ ☆

FISHERMAN'S SEAFOOD MARKET, INC.
Route 18
Grasonville, Maryland
301/827-7323

Business Season: April through October

Hours: 8 AM to 6 PM, 7 days

Carry Out Only

Dockage Available: Kent Narrows

Crab Cookery: soft crabs, crab meat picked on the premises, and live or steamed crabs by the bushel

Heading east on Route 301, immediately after crossing the Kent Narrows Bridge, make the first right and continue straight ahead. You are now face to face with the Fisherman's Seafood Market, Inc. This is our first stop on Kent Narrows and often the first is last, as delighted patrons return time and time again and may even travel hundreds of miles to get fresh crabs at Fisherman's Seafood. This is a full service seafood market where the scenery is an everchanging blend of the Bay's watermen and boating life.

CAPT. JIM'S SEAFOOD KETTLE

Route 50
Queenstown, Maryland
301/827-7488

Business Season: all year

Hours: open daily at 11 AM

Eat In/Carry Out

Crab Cookery: steamed crabs cooked to order with J.O.
Seasoning

Capt. Jim's Seafood Kettle is located 10 minutes from the Bay Bridge. The Smith family, who runs the place, says, "If you want crabs, we will have them." That's what they say in the yellow pages and on their business card, and if you ask, they say it again, "If you want crabs, we will have them!"

WYE RIVER SEAFOOD

Route 50
Wye Mills, Maryland
301/820-2302

Business Season: year round

Hours: closed Sunday, 6 AM to 6 PM daily

Carry Out Only

Crab Cookery: hard crabs, live crabs, soft crabs, and steamed crabs

Bob Gibson, owner of Wye River Seafood, says: "From our farm stand you may enjoy fresh, locally grown tomatoes, cukes, strawberries, peppers, and asparagus. A one pound bag of seafood seasoning is given free with each bushel of crabs purchased." Need more?

COOPER'S "CRAB SHACK"

Route 50
Easton, Maryland
301/822-0471

Business Season: April through November

Hours: Monday through Friday—9 AM to 6 PM, Saturday and Sunday—9 AM to 8 PM

Carry Out Only

Fly: Easton Airport

Crab Cookery: live or steamed crabs, hard or soft crabs, wholesale or retail crabs, caters to crab feasts, and J.O. Spice

A seafood counter case has replaced the three tables that filled this tiny mid-shore crab house located across from the Easton Airport. John and Dorothy Cooper have been serving hot, tasty steamed crabs for over 25 years.

THE SALTY OYSTER

Route 33, St. Michaels Road
St. Michaels, Maryland
301/745-5151

Business Season: all year

Hours: 11:30 AM to 10:30 PM

Eat In/Carry Out

Crab Cookery: Chesapeake Bay steamed crabs, caters crab feasts, crab soup, crab imperial, soft crabs, and crab salad

Edward Higgins and sons offer their fare in the "St. Michaels' tradition," which is tasty. They serve hard crabs and seafood in a relaxed air-conditioned atmosphere. Adjoining the restaurant, you will find a complete seafood market with all types of seafood delicacies prepared for you to take out on your trip home.

94

THE CRAB CLAW
Navy Point
St. Michaels, Maryland
301/745-2900

Business Season: March 15th to November 25th

Hours: 11 AM to 10 PM

Eat In/Carry Out

Dockage Available: Miles River

Crab Cookery: crab claws, vegetable crab soup, cream of crab soup; crabs—all ways: hot, steamed, and seasoned—"If he don't kick we don't cook"

There are many things one can do in St. Michaels, Maryland including taking boat runs up the Miles River, riding the board walk trains for sightseeing this old historic town, and even taking in the Chesapeake Bay Maritime Museum which is located right next door to the Crab Claw.

The Crab Claw opened in 1965 and consists of two upstairs dining rooms and a downstairs open-air patio overlooking the water. Each table affords a grand scenic view of St. Michaels Harbor.

BIG AL'S SEAFOOD MARKET
302 North Talbot Street
St. Michaels, Maryland
Retail: 301/745-3151 Wholesale: 301/745-2637

Business Season: all year

Hours: Monday through Saturday—5:30 AM to 11 PM
Sunday—5:30 to 10 PM

Carry Out Only

Crab Cookery: hard crabs, live or steamed crabs, crab cake, soft shell crabs, and crab meat

Open since 1978, Big Al's is in downtown St. Michaels and has an excellent crab cook, Allan Poore, who owns the place and creates fabulous steamed crabs. Ours were "melt-in-the-mouth delicious" and we suggest you try "Big Al's" own specially blended crab seasoning.

TOWN CREEK RESTAURANT AND MARINA
Tilghman Street
Oxford, Maryland
301/226-5131

Business Season: April to November

Hours: Sunday through Thursday—11 AM to 9 PM, Friday and Saturday—11 AM to 10 PM

Eat In/Carry Out

Dockage Available: Town Creek

Crab Cookery: steamed local crabs

Located at the foot of Tilghman Street next to the Oxford Boat Yard, the Town Creek Restaurant and Marina serves steamed crabs on two all new outside decks, one upstairs and one downstairs. Take your pick for sitting and pick the crab for eating!

PIER STREET RESTAURANT
Pier Street
Oxford, Maryland
301/226-5411

Business Season: April to November

Hours: 11 AM to 10 PM, 7 days

Eat In/Carry Out

Dockage Available: Tred Avon River

Crab Cookery: crab soup, crab cakes, and hard or soft crabs

Pier Street, located on the historic Tred Avon River, proudly states: "We choose only the finest of hand-picked local river crabs." This eatery is a complete riverside restaurant and marina—all this in perhaps one of the more beautiful settings on the Chesapeake Bay.

POP'S MARKET
Route 50
Trappe, Maryland
301/476-3900

Business Season: May 15th to October 15th

Hours: 9 AM to 9 PM daily

Carry Out Only

Crab Cookery: hard or soft crabs, live or steamed crabs, and crab meat

At Pop's...potatoes and pumpkins are some of the local produce sold at this delightful roadside market. Fresh picked vegetables and fruits are displayed on a large wood counter built onto the farm tractor. Meanwhile, the day's sea catch is available and kept fresh in a convenient walk-in cooler. Inquire about bushel sales and the house recipe for steamed crabs. Pop may give you his secret!

KOOL ICE AND SEAFOOD
110 Washington Street
Cambridge, Maryland
301/228-2300

Business Season: open all year

Hours: Monday through Saturday—8 AM to 6 PM

Carry Out Only

Crab Cookery: wholesale and retail steamed crabs, dozen and bushel sales, specializes in Maryland's Choptank River crabs, and seasoning is available in 50 lb. bags

Crab meat is picked daily at this eastern shore crab picking and packing plant and packed and labeled "Kool Brand." This is where the commercial crabber unloads his daily catch.

THE J. M. CLAYTON COMPANY
Commerce Street
Cambridge, Maryland
301/228-1661

Business Season: all year

Hours: Monday through Friday—8 AM to 5 PM, Saturday winter hours—8 AM to noon, Saturday summer hours—8 AM to 5 PM, closed Sunday

Carry Out Only

Dockage Available: "Clayton's Corner" on Cambridge Creek

Crab Cookery: live, steamed, crab meat, and shucked oysters

The J. M. Clayton Company began in Hoopersville, Maryland in 1890. Later, in 1920, the company moved to Cambridge. The great grandfather of the current owner of Clayton crabbed in a log canoe named "Epicure." From humble beginnings, a family tradition grew into one of the first establishments to pick and pack crabs in the state of Maryland. Today, continuing the family tradition, Clayton produces "Epicure Quality Chesapeake Bay Seafood."

TODD SEAFOODS, INC.
400 Cherry Street
Cambridge, Maryland
301/228-1400

Business Season: May to October

Hours: Monday to Saturday—8 AM to 5 PM

Carry Out Only

Dockage Available: Cambridge Creek

Crab Cookery: crab meat, live crabs, and steamed Maryland crabs by the dozen or the bushel spiced with J.O. Seasoning

The convenient walk-up window at Todd Seafoods, Inc. has been open for carry out service since 1948. Todd is located on Cambridge Creek at the foot of Cherry Street.

Festivals & Feasts

A bounty of seafood festivals surround the Bay. Some of the more notable are the Annual Crab Trot held in Virginia Beach every October, the J. Millard Tawes Crab and Clam Bake held each July, and the Labor Day favorite, the National Hard Crab Derby. The latter two festivals are held in the tiny town of Crisfield, the crab capital of the world, located on the lower end of the Maryland eastern shore. The Hard Crab Derby has gained national recognition and has become a major attraction to the area. There's a beauty contest, fishing contest, boat regatta, crab cooking contest, and a crab pickin' contest, not to mention the crab race itself which includes entries from Hawaii and Alaska. Anyone can enter to enjoy a little of the past and a part of today in this charming eastern shore village.

Equally popular for crab eaters is the backyard crab feast; the requirements are few. A crab feast consists of a heaping supply of hard crabs steamed to a bright red and plenty of cold beer. Crabs are usually served on a table covered with newspapers; the only utensils needed are paring knives and mallets. Complete your feast with corn-on-the-cob, tomatoes, friends, neighbors, and a hot, lazy, summer afternoon.

A tradition of fresh and tasty crabs reigns supreme here.

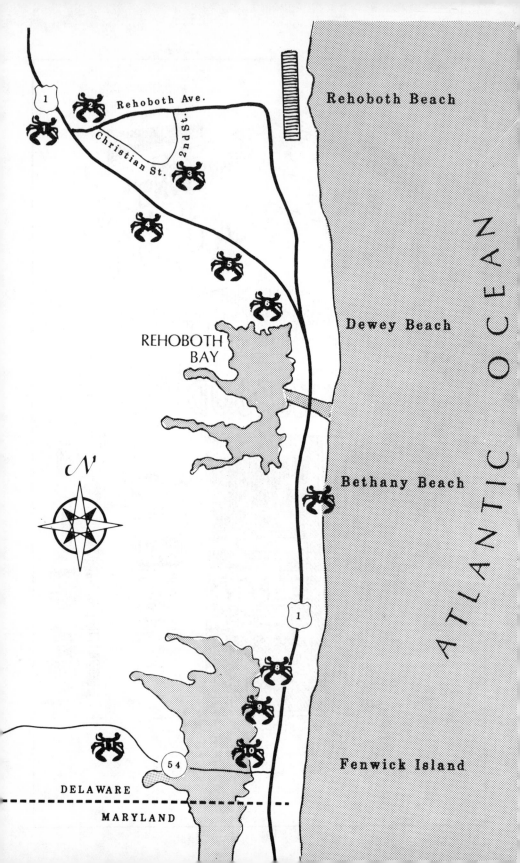

Rehoboth Ave.

2nd St.

Christian St.

Rehoboth Beach

REHOBOTH
BAY

Dewey Beach

Bethany Beach

ATLANTIC OCEAN

Fenwick Island

DELAWARE

MARYLAND

Crab Shore

REHOBOTH BEACH, DELAWARE

1. The Happy Crab Inn
2. The Crab Cafe
3. Dinner Bell Inn
4. The Crab House
5. Brown's Seafood
6. Crabbers' Cove
7. Garfield Plaza Crab House
8. Coastal Seafood Specialties, Inc.
9. Fenwick Crab House
10. Tom & Terry's Seafood
11. Mullin's Market and Country Crab Den

THE HAPPY CRAB INN
Route 1
Rehoboth Beach, Delaware
302/227-2225

Business Season: all year

Hours: 11 AM to 10:30 PM

Eat In/Carry Out

Crab Cookery: crab cakes, sautéed crab lumps, mushroom caps stuffed with crab meat, soft shell crabs, the happy crab and hot steamed crabs

The Happy Crab Inn is located just north of Rehoboth Beach. Chuck, Dee, and Cindy Stevens invite you to visit a new addition—the Happy Crab's Outside Inn. Here you can enjoy the "The Happy Crab," a hard shell crab, steamed, dipped in a beer batter and fried to a delicious golden crisp.

THE CRAB CAFE
95 Rehoboth Avenue
Rehoboth, Delaware
302/227-3877

Business Season: April to November

Hours: 11:30 AM to 11 PM

Eat In/Carry Out

Crab Cookery: crabs to take out by the dozen or bushel, cooked or uncooked

You may eat inside the restaurant or outside on the patio. The Crab Cafe is always a favorite stop when we visit Rehoboth Beach. Patrons rave about the crab feast with all the crabs and corn they can eat. A favorite place to sit is at the canopied sidewalk cafe, which offers a ringside seat to the sights and sounds of this delightful oceanside community.

DINNER BELL INN

2 Christian Street
Rehoboth Beach, Delaware
302/227-2561
302/227-2014

Business Season: July to September

Hours: 4 PM till closing, 7 days

Eat In/Carry Out

Crab Cookery: Friday and Saturday—Crab Decker: 3 steamed crabs, 1 soft shell crab, ½ lb. king crab claws, ½ lb. stone crab claws, corn-on-the-cob, and cole slaw

A country inn at the seashore, the Dinner Bell Inn is a roomy Victorian house complete with restaurant and lodging. A new addition is the crab deck, where you can enjoy hot crabs in comfortable surroundings.

THE CRAB HOUSE

Route 1
Rehoboth Beach, Delaware
302/227-9007

Business Season: May to October

Hours: 4 PM till closing, 7 days

Eat In/Carry Out

Crab Cookery: crabs and stone crab claws, crab imperial, and steamed crab feast Monday through Thursday includes salad bar

For the finest of fresh seafood, visit The Crab House. Freddy Voigt, your host, specializes in steamed crabs, steamed shrimp, and steamed clams, steamed to please.

BROWN'S SEAFOOD

3409 Highway #1
Rehoboth Beach, Delaware
302/227-7142

Business Season: daily from Memorial Day through mid-October, Thursday through Saturday during the winter months

Hours: Tuesday through Thursday—10 AM to 6 PM, Friday and Saturday—10 AM to 7 PM, Sunday—12 PM to 5 PM

Carry Out Only

Crab Cookery: steamed crabs from Maryland and North Carolina

Try this recipe from Brown's Seafood:

Cream of Crab Soup

1 lb. crab meat	½ stick margarine
1 can (8¾ oz.) chicken broth	5 C. half and half
1 t. dried parsley	2 T. cooking sherry
salt and pepper	½ C. + 1 T. flour

Melt margarine, stir in flour until smooth, stir in chicken broth, simmer a couple of minutes. Add milk and cook slowly, stirring constantly until thick. Don't let boil. Add sherry, crab meat, parsley, salt and pepper to taste. Remove from heat and serve.

CRABBERS' COVE

Dickinson Street on the Bay
Dewey Beach, Delaware
302/227-4888
For Carry Out Call:
302/227-6444

Business Season: May 1st to September 30th

Hours: 3 PM to 11 PM daily

Eat In/Carry Out

Dockage Available: Rehoboth Bay

Crab Cookery: "Chesapeake Bay hard shell crabs steamed with our own crab seasoning and served by the dozen, ½ dozen, or bushel." priced daily

The Crabbers' Cove has an inside dining room as well as an outside canopied deck area. Here you can enjoy both steamed crabs and the spectacular sunsets over the waters of the Rehoboth Bay.

GARFIELD PLAZA CRAB HOUSE

Garfield Parkway
Bethany Beach, Delaware
302/539-9200

Business Season: Memorial Day to Labor Day

Hours: 4 PM to 9 PM, 7 days

Eat In/Carry Out

Crab Cookery: crab meat, soft crabs, steamed crabs, crab cakes, and crab soup

Arnold Brown is your host of this completely remodeled fish market and crab house located on Main Street, one block from the beach. Don't pass up the all-you-can-eat specials on Wednesday and Friday throughout the summer season.

COASTAL SEAFOOD SPECIALTIES, INC.

Ocean Bay Plaza Shopping Center
Fenwick Island, Delaware
302/539-6607

Business Season: April 15th to October 15th

Hours: 9 AM to 9 PM, 7 days

Carry Out Only

Crab Cookery: crab meat, crab soup, lump meat crab cakes, imperial crab, Maryland steamed crabs (in season), and stone crab claws

Capt. Bob Harrell brings a special blend of crab cookery to his Fenwick Island location and we suggest you don't wait. So hurry by for hot steamed crabs, tackle and bait.

Bob gave us this specialty:

Captain Bob's Crab Cakes

5 lbs. crab meat (sift for shells)
(2 lbs. special, 2 lbs. backfin, and 1 lb. claw)

6 eggs

1 tsp. ground mustard

salt, pepper, Old Bay, minced onion—to your taste

6 to 8 oz. milk

Mix seasonings and meat with eggs. Add milk and mix. Add mayonnaise as needed to hold ingredients together. Makes approximately 25 4 oz. cakes. ENJOY!

FENWICK CRAB HOUSE
Coastal Highway
Fenwick Island, Delaware
302/539-2500

Business Season: April to October

Hours: open every day at 11 AM

Eat In/Carry Out

Crab Cookery: cream of crab soup, vegetable crab soup, stone crab by the pound, crab cakes, crab imperial, sautéed lump crab, crab and mushroom au gratin, stuffed flounder with lump crab imperial, and hot steamed crabs

A premier beach favorite for over 20 years, the Fenwick Crab House is informal and friendly. New owner, Scott Fornwalt proclaims that "the seafood we serve here is collected fresh daily from the Del-Mar-Va peninsula." A tradition of fresh and tasty crabs reigns supreme here.

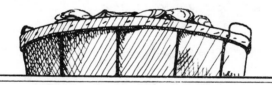

TOM & TERRY'S SEAFOOD
Route 54 and Coastal Highway
Fenwick Island, Delaware
302/539-3223

Business Season: April through December

Hours: 9 AM to 9 PM daily

Carry Out Only

Crab Cookery: hot, jumbo crabs, picked crab meat, crabs steamed or live by the dozen or bushel

Tom & Terry's Seafood presents itself as an efficiently run seafood market with a full range of crab specialties. "We guarantee everything that we sell and welcome your suggestions."

MULLIN'S MARKET AND COUNTRY CRAB DEN

Route 54
Fenwick Island, Delaware
302/436-5022

Business Season: April to November

Hours: 8 AM to 10 PM, 7 days

Eat In/Carry Out

Crab Cookery: soft or hard crabs—live or steamed

Mullin's Market and Country Crab Den can be found by turning west at the Fenwick Island traffic light and proceeding about a mile and a half. The Crab Den is a pleasant and friendly place that overlooks Little Assawoman Bay.

Fried Soft Shell Crabs

12 soft shell crabs

2 eggs, beaten

¼ cup milk

2 teaspoons salt

1 teaspoon pepper

¾ cup flour

¾ cup dry bread crumbs

Clean crabs by cutting off the face just back of the eyes. Remove the apron; remove the spongy parts (the gills, stomach, and intestines) under the points of the body covering. Rinse in cold water; drain. Combine egg, milk, salt and pepper. Combine flour and crumbs. Dip crabs in egg mixture and roll in flour-and-crumb mixture.

110

Crab

By some definitions, not a likable fellow;
Bad meanings attached to his fame.
Probably by accident
Some cynic got pinched
And gave rise
To Crab's ill-fortuned name.

For instance:
A Crab in an apple won't keep the doctor away,
A Crab that itches never gets invited to stay,
A Crab that bitches should be thrown in the bay,
But a Crab we can eat can change our whole day.

By an eater's definition, a Crab is a King
Among crustaceans, brave and bold.
That succulent meat,
Oh, so sweet,
Is worth its weight in gold.

For instance:
Crabmeat and buttered spices broiled up right,
In Crab à la King the chef reaches his height,
Crabcakes, crispy, are a wonderful sight.
Crab is the crabeaters soulful delight.

Lynne Haas

There's more to the ocean than sun and fun.
There's hot steamed crabs skillfully done.

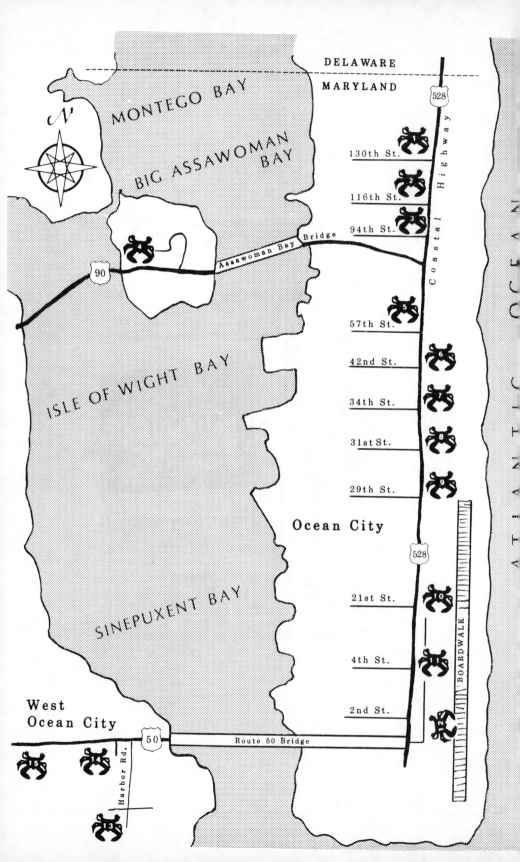

Crab Shore

OCEAN CITY, MARYLAND

1. The Crab Bag
2. House of Crabs
3. Mug and Mallet
4. Hemphill's Dock
5. Gunning's House of Seafood
6. Jim's Seafood
7. Wallace's Crab House
8. Old Shuckers Seafood Restaurant
9. P.G.N. Crab House and Restaurant
10. Phillips Crab House
11. Griffin's Seafood Market
12. Mug and Mallet
13. The Steamer
14. Mr.Bill's
15. House of Crabs

THE CRAB BAG

13005 Coastal Highway
North Ocean City, Maryland
301/524-3337

Business Season: May to September

Hours: Monday through Friday—4 PM to 11 PM, Saturday and Sunday—noon to 11:30 PM

Eat In/Carry Out

Crab Cookery: hot steamed crabs

This mustard-painted, two-story clapboard crab house can be found sandwiched between the highrises in the Montego Bay shopping area. It is one of the few remaining structures that reflect the history of this seaside settlement.

Do not miss the "Grab Bag," the daily special, which consists of home grown tomatoes, corn steamed with Maryland lobster, clams, crabs, and shrimp.

HOUSE OF CRABS

116th Street and Coastal Highway
Ocean City, Maryland
301/524-1118

Business Season: March to mid-November

Hours: 11 AM to 11 PM daily

Carry Out Only

Crab Cookery: hot steamed crabs

The House of Crabs is located in the Oyster Bay Shopping Center just across the street from the Carousel. The House of Crabs claims: "We steam the best crabs in Ocean City."

MUG AND MALLET

94th Street Shopping Plaza
Ocean City, Maryland
301/524-5959

Business Season: April to October

Hours: 11 AM to 2 AM

Eat In/Carry Out

Crab Cookery: steamed crabs, big red crabs, and soft crabs

If there were an election to nominate the best eating place for crab lovers, we would have a hard time deciding, but surely the Mug and Mallet would rank among the top choices.

HEMPHILL'S DOCK

Saltgrass Point Road
Bishopville, Maryland
301/352-3297

Business Season: March to November

Hours: 8 AM to 6 PM

Carry Out Only

Dockage Available: St. Martin's Creek

Crab Cookery: hard crabs, soft crabs, and live or steamed crabs cooked to order

Hemphill's Dock is home for the succulent seafoods of the Del-Mar-Va peninsula. I am uncertain about what attracted me the most to Hemphill's. Was it the aroma of delicious steamed crabs or the sound of screeching gulls calling me to carry out?

117

GUNNING'S HOUSE OF SEAFOOD

57th Street and Coastal Highway
Ocean City, Maryland
301/524-2007

Business Season: year round

Hours: noon to midnight daily

Eat In/Carry Out

Crab Cookery: steamed crabs the "old fashioned way"

Ed Gunnings, of Baltimore fame, opened this ocean crab house in 1978. In addition to two large dining rooms inside the restaurant, an outdoor crab deck is available for your enjoyment, weather permitting. After tasting your crabs steamed the old fashioned way, why not visit the Laugh Inn above Gunning's House of Seafood. Here you can enjoy Ocean City's only professional comedy night club featuring live stand-up comedians from New York, Los Angeles, and Washington, D.C. These talented jokesters come directly from shows such as Saturday Night Live, the Tonight Show, and the Merv Griffin Show.

· cut away face

·lift shell points & cut away gills

How to dress a softie

· cut away apron ·

118

JIM'S SEAFOOD

4204 Coastal Highway and 43rd Street
Ocean City, Maryland
301/289-9130

Business Season: all year

Hours: 10 AM to 11 PM, 7 days a week; after October, weekends only

Carry Out Only

Crab Cookery: steamed hard shell crabs, crab meat, crab cakes, crab soup, and soft shell crabs

A place known for its friendliness and warmth, Jim's Seafood is also famous for outstanding steamed crabs and maintains a year-round following of ocean area visitors. Jim's unique seasoning is largely that of Baltimore Spice, but is adapted to suit Jim's special needs. YUM!

WALLACE'S CRAB HOUSE

34th and Coastal Highway
Ocean City, Maryland
301/289-3318

Business Season: end of March to September 1st

Hours: 10 AM 'till closing

Eat In/Carry Out

Crab Cookery: hot steamed crabs, fried hard crabs, crab fluff, soft crabs, and crab imperial

On Saturday night, you may have to wait a short time to be seated at Wallace's, but the staff is eager to serve, and the delightful crabs arrive promptly. When you taste any of the crab dishes from Wallace's wide selection, you will understand the reason why "Hobie's hot 'n' ready crabs" are so popular.

OLD SHUCKERS SEAFOOD RESTAURANT

31st and Coastal Highway
Ocean City, Maryland
301/289-8591

Business Season: year round

Hours: noon 'till 10 PM

Eat In/Carry Out

Crab Cookery: hot steamed crabs from Maryland, Louisiana, and Texas

Another rainy day on your ocean holiday? Stuck indoors with the kids having you climb the walls? Steamed crabs are in order—give the Old Shuckers a call.

P.G.N. CRAB HOUSE AND RESTAURANT

29th and Coastal Highway
Ocean City, Maryland
301/289-8380

Business Season: March through December

Hours: 11 AM to 11 PM

Eat In/Carry Out

Crab Cookery: steamed crabs, crab soup, and crab cakes

On a Pretty Good Night, People Go Nuts with Pete, George, and Nick.

PHILLIPS CRAB HOUSE
21st and Philadelphia Avenue
Ocean City, Maryland
301/289-6821
Carry Out: 301/289-7747

Business Season: end of March to October

Hours: 11:30 AM to 11 PM

Eat In/Carry Out

Crab Cookery: crab finger cocktail, crab soup, backfin lump crab salad, steamed spiced crabs, crab cake sandwich, soft shell crab sandwich, red crabs, crab lumps au gratin, crab lumps sautéed with Smithfield ham, and crab Norfolk

Hard crabs and hard work are two reasons Phillips Crab House is rated among the top 100 restaurants in the country.

Brice and Shirley Phillips began in the seafood packing business in the early 1950's and in 1956 purchased a small tar-papered shack. Crabs then sold for $2 a dozen and Brice and Shirley had no idea the business would prosper the way it has today. But the crabs were cooked with care and, soon after, the Phillips established themselves as one of the most respected names in crab cooking. Today, a trip to Ocean City generally means a stop at one of the three ocean locations.

This Phillips Crab House will seat 1,400 guests in 13 dining rooms; the crab house has five kitchens and a staff of 450. Here you may enjoy a ''taste of Maryland.'' Eat crabs on antique sewing machine tables lit by tiffany lamps and colored lights filtered through stained glass windows. The ambiance is delightful and the service is excellent.

The Phillips are a proud and pleasant Eastern shore family with a reputation for hospitality, excellent food, and service that span 29 years.

GRIFFIN'S SEAFOOD MARKET
4th and Philadelphia
Ocean City, Maryland
301/289-7775

Business Season: year round

Hours: open 24 hours in season; off-season hours—open at 8 AM, closing varies

Carry Out Only

Crab Cookery: crabs—hard or soft, live or steamed; crab soup and crab claws

Crabs for breakfast? You bet, and they have been cooked to order Griffin's, available 24 hours a day for over 40 years.

MUG AND MALLET
Boardwalk and 2nd Street
Ocean City, Maryland
301/289-5995

Business Season: April to October

Hours: 11 AM to 2 AM

Eat In/Carry Out

Crab Cookery: crab cakes, soft crabs, and hot steamed crabs

At the Mug and Mallet, boardwalk crab feasts are provided on uniq tables built to look like boats.

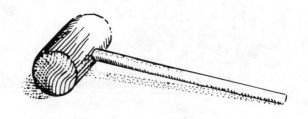

THE STEAMER

Sunset Avenue and Harbor Road
West Ocean City, Maryland
301/289-4463

Business Season: all year

Hours: 9:30 AM to 8 PM daily

Eat In/Carry Out

Dockage Available: at the head of the harbor

Crab Cookery: fresh, live or steamed Maryland blue crabs, red crabs, stone crab claws, crab cakes, and homemade crab soup

Did you ever arrive at the ocean to look for a place away from the beach—a place to spend a few hours eating good seafood and drinking beer, one that offers a unique atmosphere and is just minutes from the boardwalk? The Steamer is that kind of place. Captain Jim Whaley features everything that goes in a steamer basket. You can sit down to enjoy your purchase at a colorful outside crab eating area.

MR. BILL'S
Corner of Route 50 and 611
West Ocean City, Maryland
301/289-4190

Business Season: May 1st to September 15th

Hours: 11 AM to 11 PM daily

Carry Out Only

Crab Cookery: steamed or live hard shell crabs

There's more to the ocean than sun and fun. There's hot steamed crabs skillfully done...from Mr. Bill's.

HOUSE OF CRABS
U.S. Route 50
Ocean City, Maryland
301/289-8778

Business Season: March to mid-November

Hours: 11 AM to 11 PM daily

Eat In/Carry Out

Crab Cookery: hard steamed crabs, crab soup, crab cakes, crab fluff, and soft crabs

Over the years, the House of Crabs has perfected a steaming technique which provides quality crabs of superior flavor.

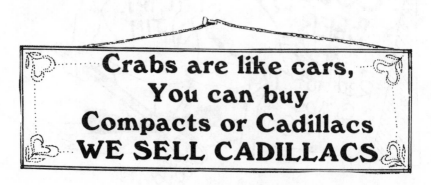

Crabs are like cars,
You can buy
Compacts or Cadillacs
WE SELL CADILLACS

J.O. Spice and Cure Company was founded in 1946 by James Ozzle Strigle, a native of Tangier Island which sits in the middle of the Chesapeake Bay. James Ozzle began with a small meat curing business on the tiny island. As his business developed, he recognized that steaming was the favorite method of preparing hard shell crabs and that seasoning enhanced the crab's flavor. He knew, too, that the seasoning varied from region to region. With this understanding, he introduced a product to suit individual tastes—J.O. Brand Seafood Seasoning. J.O.'s special blend contains salt, mustard, red pepper, celery, paprika, cracked red pepper, black pepper, mace, and cinnamon. For those who prefer a change, J.O. #1 and J.O. #2 are offered.

Today, more than 400 barrels of J.O. Brand Seafood Seasoning are sold each week and it has become a permanent accompaniment for steamed crabs and is part of a Bay tradition.

J.O. welcomes the public from 8:30 AM to 4:00 PM, Monday through Friday, year round, at 8236 Hammonds Ferry Road in Linthicum, Maryland.

The land is a flat terrain with sandy soil and
marshes that abound with wildlife and wildflowers.

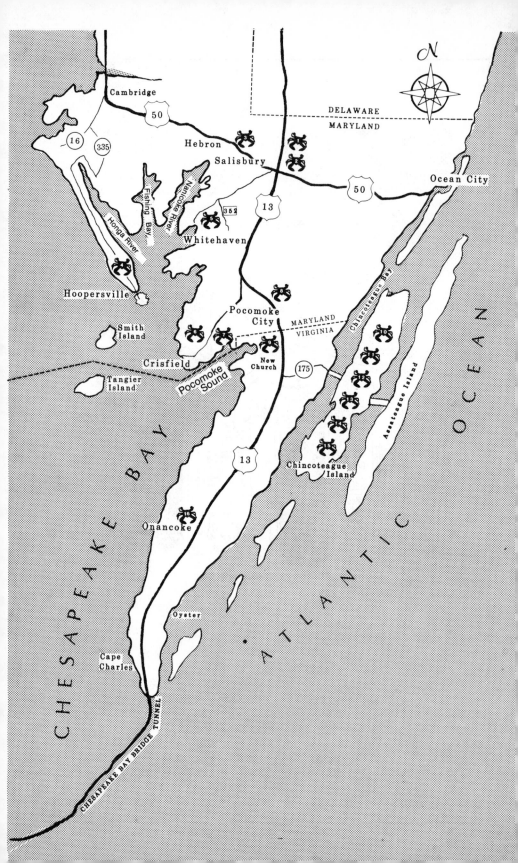

Lower Bay
Crab Country

MD & VA EASTERN SHORE

1. Crab Pot
2. Mug and Mallet
3. Mel's Produce and Seafood
4. Rippons Brothers
5. The Red Roost
6. Crisfield Elks 1044
7. Side Street Seafood Market
8. Big Apple Market
9. Susan's Seafood
10. McCready's Seafood
11. Landmark Crab House
12. Don's Seafood Restaurant
13. Mason Seafood Company
14. Carpenter's Seafood, Inc.
15. Melvin's Seafood
16. J & C Seafood

CRAB POT
U.S. 13 North and Naylor Mill Road
Salisbury, Maryland
301/543-CRAB

Business Season: all year

Hours: Monday through Thursday—9 AM to 7 PM; Friday, Saturday, and Sunday—9 AM to 8 PM

Carry Out Only

Crab Cookery: hard or soft crabs, live or steamed crabs

To many, the lower Bay crab country is a place where folks come to camp and fish and crab. The land is a flat terrain with sandy soil and marshes that abound with wildlife and wildflowers. The huge peninsula is dotted with islands and tiny fishing villages.

The Crab Pot is a roadside market that caters to the many travelers using busy U.S. 13. We suggest you try them for crabs, fish, shrimp and year-round produce. At the Crab Pot, "We steam and clean."

MUG AND MALLET
Route 13
Salisbury, Maryland
301/546-3113

Business Season: all year

Hours: Monday through Saturday—11 AM to 10 PM, Sunday—12:30 PM to 10 PM

Eat In/Carry Out

Crab Cookery: Maryland blue crabs steamed with the unique Mug and Mallet seasoning, crab soup, crab cake, soft crab, crab quiche, and crab imperial

To bait your appetite, the Mug and Mallet suggests you consider their crab cake "homemade and delicious." You might choose, instead, a soft crab batter-dipped and deep fried or, perhaps, Maryland blue crabs with the unique Mug and Mallet seasoning, or there's "Neptune's steamed seafood platter" featuring three shrimp, three clams, three oysters, stone claws, and two blue crabs.

MEL'S PRODUCE AND SEAFOOD

U.S. Route 50
Hebron, Maryland
301/742-9252

Business Season: year round

Hours: 8:30 AM to 7:30 PM daily

Carry Out Only

Crab Cookery: soft, live, or steamed crabs with Baltimore Spice

Mel's Produce and Seafood offers a delightful blend of mid-shore crab cookery and, along with a year round produce business, supplies customers with fresh fish, clams, oysters, and shrimp.

The following is Mel's favorite recipe for crab cakes:

Crab Cakes

1 lb. crab meat	1 T. parsley flakes
2 large eggs	1 t. ground mustard
1 T. Old Bay Seasoning	1½ C. cracker meal

Mix all ingredients together and form into 6 patties. Fry in oil. Delicious.

RIPPONS BROTHERS
Hoopersville, Maryland
301/397-3200

Business Season: April to November

Hours: sun up to sun down

Eat In/Carry Out

Dockage Available: Honga River

Crab Cookery: hard crabs, soft crabs, and crab meat

Rippons Brothers are packers and shippers of fine seafood. On-location crab feasts are offered in the enclosed pavillion at the water's edge. Guests are welcome by the busload.

Call Chan, Jr. for your feast schedule.

THE RED ROOST
Whitehaven, Maryland
301/546-5443

Business Season: April 15th to October 15th

Hours: Memorial Day to Labor Day: Monday through Saturday—5 PM to 10 PM; Sunday—3 PM to 9 PM; April 15th to Memorial Day and Labor Day to October 15th: Wednesday through Saturday—6 PM to 10 PM; Sunday—4 PM to 8 PM

Eat In/Carry Out

Crab Cookery: hot steamed crabs and fried chicken

Located near historic Whitehaven, The Red Roost once produced Perdue chickens. Frank Palmer, Jr. rebuilt the Red Roost in 1971 and now features an all-you-can-eat crab feast with fried chicken on the side, hush puppies, and corn-on-the-cob.

CRISFIELD ELKS 1044
Route 413
Crisfield, Maryland
301/968-3051

Business Season: April to November

Hours: 1 PM to 6 PM and 7 PM to closing daily except
Sundays

Eat In/Carry Out

Crab Cookery: steamed hard crabs

Crisfield is a little town between Tangier Sound and Pocomoke Sound
on the Atlantic side of the mouth of the Chesapeake Bay, a prime location
for crabs. For years, the public has been invited to enjoy tasty, fresh crabs at
the Elk's Club. Stop in. The members are anxious to serve you and you will
find this one of the best values around on steamed crabs and good eatin'.

Avocados Stuffed with Crab Meat

1 pound crab meat

2 tablespoons butter

2 tablespoons flour

1 cup milk

¼ teaspoon salt

Dash pepper

¼ teaspoon Worcestershire sauce

2 tablespoons chopped pimiento

2 tablespoons chopped olives

3 ripe avocados

¼ cup grated cheddar cheese

Remove any shell or cartilage from crab meat. Melt butter; blend in
flour. Add milk slowly and cook until thick and smooth, stirring constantly.
Add seasonings, pimiento, olives, and crab meat. Cut avocados in half;
remove seeds. Fill centers with crab mixture; sprinkle cheese over top of each
avocado. Place in a well-greased baking pan. Bake in a moderate oven, 350°
F., for 20 to 25 minutes or until brown. Serves 6.

SIDE STREET SEAFOOD MARKET
10th and Main Street
Crisfield, Maryland
301/968-2442

Business Season: April through the end of November

Hours: upstairs—11 AM until everyone leaves, downstairs—
9 AM to 10 PM

Eat In/Carry Out

Crab Cookery: steamed crabs and soft crabs

Allen Tyler and Jim Dodson are your hosts at the Side Street Seafood Market, "your complete seafood processing center." Downstairs, you will find a raw bar carry out; upstairs is an outdoor dining area. A peaceful, unspoiled atmosphere is most attractive in this neighborhood of seafood warehouses and harbor boats.

Barbecued Crab Sandwiches

½ pound crab meat

¼ cup chopped spring onion

½ cup chopped celery

3 tablespoons melted butter

¼ teaspoon salt

Dash pepper

2 whole bay leaves

2 whole cloves

2 teaspoons soy sauce

2 teaspoons Worcestershire sauce

1 chicken bouillon cube

½ cup tomato juice

2 tablespoons chopped parsley

6 large buttered rolls

Remove any shell or cartilage from crab meat. Cook onion and celery in butter until tender. Add seasonings, bouillon cube, and tomato juice. Simmer for 5 minutes. Remove bay leaves and cloves. Add parsley and crab meat; heat. Serve on rolls. Serves 6.

BIG APPLE MARKET
U.S. 13
Pocomoke City, Maryland
301/957-1151

Business Season: year round

Hours: Monday to Thursday—8:30 AM to 8:30 PM, Friday and Saturday—8:30 AM to 9:30 PM, Sunday—9:00 AM to 8:30 PM

Carry Out Only

Crab Cookery: crabs—steamed or live, hard or soft, wholesale and retail

The Big Apple Market boasts of "lots of crabs and lots of apples." That's what they had late last summer when we paid a visit. From the road, you would think they sold only crabs and apples; there is much more to see. The Big Apple is a year round market that features the best of the locally grown produce and freshly caught seafood. Stop and look around.

SUSAN'S SEAFOOD
Route 13
New Church, Virginia
804/824-5545

Business Season: all year

Hours: 8 AM to 8 PM daily

Carry Out Only

Crab Cookery: soft crabs, live crabs, and crabs steamed with Baltimore Spice Seasoning

She sells
soft shells
on the sea
shore.
Try one
and you'll
surely want more.

McCREADY'S SEAFOOD
Beach Road
Chincoteague, Virginia
804/336-5655

Business Season: April to September

Hours: Monday through Saturday—11 AM to 9 PM, closed Sunday

Eat In/Carry Out

Crab Cookery: steamed crabs

. . .screened eat-in area, take-outs, and phone-in orders. . .phone 'em, take 'em, eat 'em.

Annie's Hostess Crab Delight

1 lb. crab meat	2 c. milk
¼ c. onion, minced	3 c. *cooked* rice
¼ c. parsley, chopped	1 c. grated sharp cheese
¼ c. pimiento, chopped	1 tsp. Worcestershire sauce
3 eggs, slightly beaten	

Cook rice and drain. Gently combine all ingredients. Place in buttered 8 x 11 baking pan. Bake 35-45 min. at 325 degrees. Cut into squares and serve with Shrimp Sauce. Recipe below.

Shrimp Sauce

2 cans cream of shrimp soup
1 c. sour cream
1 tsp. lemon juice
½ c. cooked shrimp, (optional) chopped

Blend all ingredients and warm slowly over low heat, preferably in iron skillet. Do not boil. Serves 8-10.

LANDMARK CRAB HOUSE
Main Street
Landmark Plaza
Chincoteague, Virginia
804/336-5552

Business Season: March to November

Hours: Tuesday through Saturday—5 PM to 10 PM, Sunday—1 PM to 9 PM, closed Monday

Eat In Only

Dockage Available: Chincoteague Channel

Crab Cookery: steamed crabs and clams

A stroll through memory lane is what comes to mind as you step into this antique waterfront lounge. The Old Brunswick Bar of 1897 was brought from Chicago and refurbished especially for the Landmark Crab House.

DON'S SEAFOOD RESTAURANT
Main Street
Chincoteague, Virginia
804/336-5715

Business Season: May to November

Hours: 5 AM to 10 PM, 7 days

Eat In/Carry Out

Dockage Available: Chincoteague Channel

Crab Cookery: hard or soft crabs and live or steamed crabs

You will enjoy the nautical decor of Don's Seafood Restaurant. Located on Main Street, it is fast becoming one of the most popular gathering spots on the Chincoteague Island. A casual, yet tasteful atmosphere allows you "to get down" to eating mouth-watering crab specialties. After your meal, you may try Chattie's Lounge above the restaurant for cocktails and dancing.

MASON SEAFOOD COMPANY
544 South Main Street
Chincoteague, Virginia
804/336-6900

Business Season: all year

Hours: 8 AM to 7 PM, 7 days

Carry Out Only

Dockage Available: Chincoteague Channel

Crab Cookery: soft shell crabs, live or steamed crabs,
homemade crab cakes, and deviled crabs

Virginia is a state split by the Chesapeake Bay. While the bulk of the land area is west of the Bay, a small portion adjoins Maryland on the Eastern Shore. This is a place where folks come to relax and breathe the fresh sea air. Its a place to camp and crab. On the Atlantic side sits tiny Chincoteague Island, a wildly beautiful area formed by a string of barrier islands which offer excellent beaches, pine forests and wildlife marshes. Each visit we take here means a stop at Mason Seafood Company, operated by Tommy and Donna Mason. This popular island market supplies visitors with outstanding seafood delights.

CARPENTER'S SEAFOOD, INC.
P.O. Box 73
Chincoteague, Virginia
804/336-6956

Business Season: April to September

Hours: 8 AM to 8 PM daily

Carry Out Only

Crab Cookery: live hard crabs, crabmeat, and shucked oysters

Jim and Walt Carpenter have operated their seafood market since 1946. They are typical of the Chesapeake Bay watermen who daily fish in the area. The day's catch is stocked in the cooler and sold from the market. They claim, "We know many of the island's great spots."

MELVIN'S SEAFOOD

Bebe Street
Chincoteague, Virginia
804/336-3003

Business Season: year around

Hours: sun up to dark

Carry Out Only

Crab Cookery: live or steamed crabs

Chincoteague is a tiny island fishing village. It has an abundance of natural wildlife in the national wildlife refuge. Thousands of people come to the island each year to use the diverse recreational facilities. Robert Melvin's backyard crab house caters to the people who come to enjoy the beauty of Chincoteague and love to eat crabs.

J & C SEAFOOD

Main Street
Onancock, Virginia
804/787-7478

Business Season: all year

Hours: sun up to sun down, closed Sundays

Carry Out Only

Crab Cookery: live crabs, steamed crabs, soft crabs, and crab meat

J & C Seafood is located on a large peninsula where the livelihood of the people is provided by the land and sea. In an area where such an abundance of seafood is available, J & C will provide you the same outstanding fresh crabs that they offer the local people. Visit them and find out for yourself.

The tidewater area is one of the richest in the country when it comes to the availability of fresh seafood.

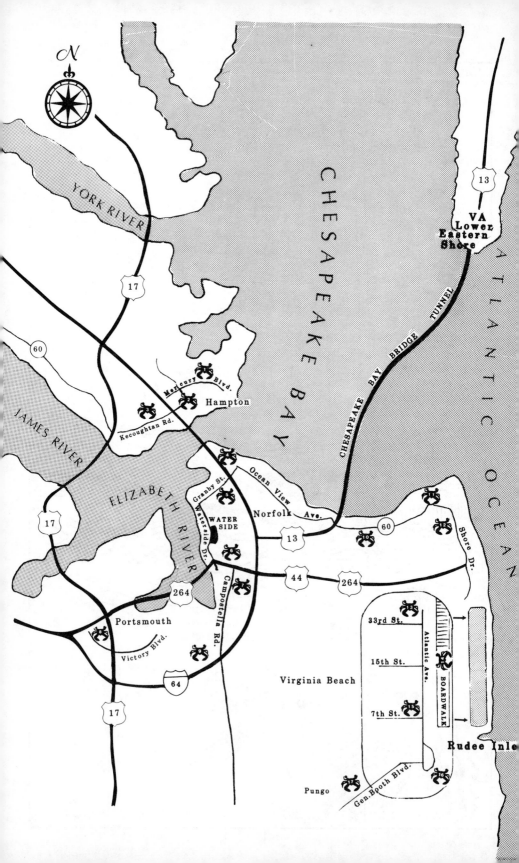

She Crab Country

1. King Crab Co.
2. Phillips Seafood Co.
3. McKoy's Seafood Kitchen
4. Willoughby Inn
5. Hagan Seafood Company
6. Phillips Waterside
7. Channel Crab Company
8. Wicker's Crab and Seafood Co.
9. Chesapeake Bay Crab House
10. Seafood Shack
11. Captain Kidd's Seafood
12. Shoreline Seafood
13. Captain John's Crab House
14. Ocean Crab House
15. Captain Kidd's Crab House
16. The Lighthouse
17. Captain Kidd's Restaurant and Marina

KING CRAB CO.
504 Mercury Boulevard
Hampton, Virginia
804/722-3966

Business Season: all year

Hours: Tuesday through Saturday—10 AM to 7 PM,
Sunday—12 noon to 6 PM

Carry Out Only

Crab Cookery: live and steamed crabs by the dozen or by the
bushel, wholesale or retail

King Crab Company is a roadside seafood market carrying fresh
seafood favorites. This day's offering included Virginia filet of flounder,
croaker, and special large trout filets, as well as live crabs by the dozen or by
the bushel.

PHILLIPS SEAFOOD CO.
Bassette and Armistead Avenue
Hampton, Virginia
804/838-2887

Business Season: all year

Hours: 11 AM to 11 PM, 7 days a week

Carry Out Only

Crab Cookery: retail fish and crabs, steamed hard crabs,
Hampton crab cake with tomato sauce, and deviled crabs

John Phillips, proprietor, informs us that all of his seafood delights are
delivered "fresh from the sea to our market."

McKOY'S SEAFOOD KITCHEN
911 Kecoughtan Road
Newport News, Virginia
804/244-6191

Business Season: all year

Hours: 9 AM to 6 PM

Carry Out Only

Crab Cookery: hard, soft, live, and steamed crabs

McKoy's Seafood Kitchen has taken 20 years of seafood experience and wrapped it into one neat package. They offer delicious seafood and barbecue dishes and bring to you the ocean's finest in fresh seafood. They "invite you to plunge with us in our little ocean in the city."

WILLOUGHBY INN
1534 West Ocean View Avenue
Norfolk, Virginia
804/480-0226

Business Season: May to October

Hours: 8 AM to 2 AM, 7 days

Eat In/Carry Out

Crab Cookery: steamed hard crabs

At Willoughby Inn you can relax in a nautical atmosphere, dressed casually, and enjoy the succulent seafood delicacies which grace your table.

HAGAN SEAFOOD COMPANY

4226 Granby Street
(foot of Granby Street Bridge)
Norfolk, Virginia
804/627-0743

Business Season: all year

Hours: 10 AM to 6 PM, closed Sunday and Monday

Carry Out Only

Crab Cookery: soft crabs, steamed crabs, and live crabs

The tidewater area is one of the richest in the country when it comes to the availability of fresh seafood. Hagan Seafood, which opens its doors at the foot of the Granby Street Bridge, provides not only a picturesque setting but a stocked seafood market handling top quality fresh seafood daily.

Cream of Crab Soup

1 pound crab meat

1 chicken bouillon cube

1 cup boiling water

¼ cup chopped onion

¼ cup butter

3 tablespoons flour

¼ teaspoon celery salt

1 teaspoon salt

Dash pepper

1 quart milk

Chopped parsley

Remove any shell or cartilage from crab meat. Dissolve bouillon cube in water. Cook onion in butter until tender. Blend in flour and seasonings. Add milk and bouillon gradually; cook until thick, stirring constantly. Add crab meat; heat. Garnish with parsley sprinkled over the top. Sherry is optional. Serves 6.

PHILLIPS WATERSIDE

333 Waterside Drive
Norfolk, Virginia
804/627-6600

Business Season: year round

Hours: 11 AM to 11 PM, 7 days a week, closed Christmas Day

Eat In/Carry Out

Dockage Available: Elizabeth River

Crab Cookery: crabs can be purchased from the raw and steam station, the seafood market, and the deck side

Tidewater's festive waterside marketplace, the Norfolk waterfront, is home to Phillips' newest dockside location.

Add Phillips' Victorian decor and excellent steamed crabs to a colorful marketplace and bustling waterfront, and you have the sure ingredients for a joyful experience.

After a meal at Phillips, you may want to take in the many sides of Waterside. There are inside activities, outside activities, sideline festivities with jugglers, musicians, art exhibits, and, of course, a beautiful view of the Elizabeth River.

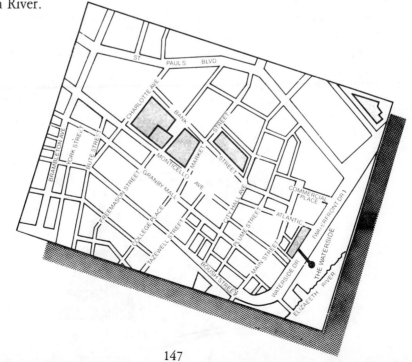

CHANNEL CRAB COMPANY

714 Stapleton Street
Norfolk, Virginia
804/622-3724

Business Season: all year

Hours: weekdays—10 AM to 8:30 PM, Friday and Saturday—10 AM to 9:30 PM

Carry Out Only

Crab Cookery: steamed crabs, fried crabs, and deviled crabs

Channel Crab Company can be found just off interstate 264 at the intersection of Westminster Avenue and Stapleton Street. The Jones' family specializes in deviled, fried, steamed, and fresh crabs.

WICKER'S CRAB AND SEAFOOD CO.

3138 Victory Blvd.
Portsmouth, Virginia
804/487-4201

Business Season: all year

Hours: 11 AM to 11 PM, 7 days

Carry Out Only

Crab Cookery: hard and soft crabs, live and steamed crabs, and deviled and fried crabs

Considered by many to be one of the best carry outs in the Portsmouth area, Mr. Wicker has been cooking crabs for more than 12 years. Wicker's could become your favorite seafood market. Try it.

CHESAPEAKE BAY CRAB HOUSE

2592 Campostella Road
Chesapeake, Virginia
804/545-0653

Business Season: all year

Hours: 1 PM to 8 PM, 7 days

Eat In/Carry Out

Crab Cookery: fresh steamed crabs, crab meat, deviled crab, wholesale and retail crabs, and Baltimore Spice

For delicious seafood in the tidewater area, try the Chesapeake Bay Crab House which offers fresh crab meat and steamed crabs daily. This crab house is located opposite the South Drive-In Movie.

SEAFOOD SHACK

2302 East Ocean View Avenue
Norfolk, Virginia
804/480-0606

Business Season: all year

Hours: 10 AM to 6 PM

Carry Out Only

Crab Cookery: crabs—live, steamed, by the dozen, or by the bushel

Just west of the Lynnhaven Inlet, the Seafood Shack offers fresh seafood daily as well as bait and tackle, crab nets, and crab lines.

CAPTAIN KIDD'S SEAFOOD

3232 Shore Drive
Virginia Beach, Virginia
804/481-7528

Business Season: May through October

Hours: weekdays—3 PM to 11 PM, Friday and Saturday—3 PM to 12 PM, Sunday—3 PM to 11 PM

Eat In/Carry Out

Crab Cookery: steamed hard crabs

The seafood lover has many specials to choose from at Captain Kidd's. One favorite is a steamed seafood platter which consists of eight oysters, eight clams, three hard shell crabs, and all the shrimp you can eat.

SHORELINE SEAFOOD

2917 Shore Drive
Virginia Beach, Virginia
804/481-3642

Business Season: open daily

Hours: 10 AM to 6 PM

Carry Out Only

Crab Cookery: steamed crabs, crab meat, and soft crabs

The menu today listed shrimp, lobster tails, king crab legs, crabs, fish, oysters, and scallops. Our selection, of course, was crab, mighty good.

150

CAPTAIN JOHN'S CRAB HOUSE

33rd and Atlantic Avenue
Virginia Beach, Virginia
804/425-6263

Business Season: all year

Hours: 11 AM to 11 PM

Eat In/Carry Out

Crab Cookery: steamed hard crabs, crab imperial, crab soup,
crab au gratin, and crab cakes

The "old stand-by" since 1975, Captain John's Crab House serves us
seafood caught daily on their own trawler. Try anything on the extensive
menu and you'll be more than satisfied.

OCEAN CRAB HOUSE

15th Street and Ocean Front
Virginia Beach, Virginia
804/428-6186

Business Season: year round

Hours: noon to 10 PM daily

Eat In/Carry Out

Crab Cookery: fried soft shell crabs, deviled crabs, crab cakes,
and steamed crabs

Steamed shrimp and steamed crabs are a house specialty at the Ocean
Crab House. The seafood buffet offers a wonderful assortment of fare along
with live nightly entertainment.

CAPTAIN KIDD'S CRAB HOUSE
706 Atlantic Avenue
Virginia Beach, Virginia
804/428-2073

Business Season: May through October

Hours: Monday through Thursday—3 PM to 11 PM, Friday and Saturday—3 PM to 12 AM, Sunday—3 PM to 11 PM

Eat In/Carry Out

Crab Cookery: steamed hard crabs

Come to Captain Kidd's and have a feast! A complete selection of fresh broiled, fried, or steamed seafood is offered daily from Kidd's trawlers. In a relaxing nautical atmosphere, you will find prices you can afford and food that will make you want to come back.

Bo's Crab Gumbo

1 pound crab meat

½ cup chopped onion

½ cup chopped celery

1 clove garlic, finely chopped

¼ cup butter

2 teaspoons salt

1 teaspoon fresh thyme

¼ teaspoon sugar

1 whole bay leaf

Dash pepper

1 package (10 ounces) frozen okra, sliced

2 cans (1 pound 4 ounces each) tomatoes

1½ cups cooked rice

Remove any shell from crab meat. Cook onion, celery, and garlic in butter until tender. Add seasonings, okra, and tomatoes. Cover and simmer for 45 minutes. Remove bay leaf. Add crab meat; heat. Serve over rice. Serves 6.

THE LIGHTHOUSE
Ocean and Rudee Inlet at 1st Street
Virginia Beach, Virginia
804/428-9851

Business Season: year round, closed Christmas Day

Hours: 10 AM to 11 PM

Dockage Available: Rudee Inlet

Eat In/Carry Out

Crab Cookery: she crab soup, steamed crabs, and soft shell crabs

After mating, female blue crabs migrate to the area we call "she crab country." This migration results in a concentration of adult females in the lower Bay region.

The first inlet to the north Atlantic Ocean, after you leave the Chesapeake Bay and head south past Cape Henry, is Rudee Inlet. This is home to The Lighthouse restaurant. Enjoying The Lighthouse's she crab soup and steamed crabs is one of the treats in coming to this unique area.

CAPTAIN KIDD'S RESTAURANT AND MARINA
2272 Pungo Ferry Road
Virginia Beach, Virginia
804/426-7016

Business Season: May through October

Hours: weekdays—3 PM to 11 PM, Friday and Saturday—3 PM to 12 PM, Sunday—3 PM to 11 PM

Eat In/Carry Out

Dockage Available: Intercoastal Waterway/Pungo Ferry

Crab Cookery: steamed hard shell crabs

Take a leisurely and scenic drive through the country along the Intercoastal Waterway at the Pungo Ferry Bridge. Stop at Capt. Kidd's to enjoy a steamed crab feast with corn-on-the-cob, hush puppies, and cole slaw. Opened in 1976, this eatery has two large rustic rooms with dark wood walls and windows that offer a pleasant view of the Intercoastal Waterway. As a bonus, there is fishing from the dock, boating on the water, or picnicking on the surrounding 30 acres.

"Surrounded by natural waterways and laced with creeks and inlets, the northern neck area of the Chesapeake Bay is of natural and breathtaking beauty."

Source: Virginia Promotional Material.

154

Northern Neck

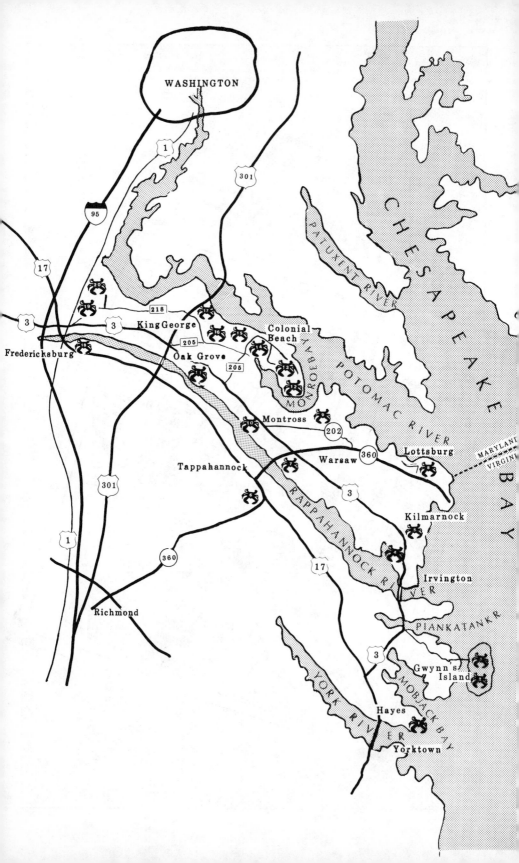

Northern Neck Seafood

1. York River Seafood Co., Inc.
2. Milford Haven Crab House of Va.
3. L. & L. Fish Market
4. Clifford Winstead's Crabs
5. Rappahannock Oyster Company
6. Tappahannock Seafood
7. Northern Neck Seafood
8. Keyser Brothers, Inc.
9. Capt. Faunce Seafood
10. Pete Allen Oyster Company and Seafood
11. Winter Harbor Seafood
12. Parker's Crab Shore
13. Steve's Seafood Restaurant
14. Pearson's Seafood
15. Wilkerson's Seafood Restaurant
16. Shady Lane Seafood Carry-Out
17. Roy's Seafood
18. Barefoot Green's Seafood
19. Newton Seafood
20. Bourne Seafood

YORK RIVER SEAFOOD CO., INC.
Route 2
Hayes, Virginia
804/642-2151

Business Season: all year

Hours: 5:30 AM to 5:30 PM

Carry Out Only

Dockage Available: Perrin River

Crab Cookery: live or steamed crabs and crab meat

York River Seafood Co. specializes in clams, oysters, fish, crabs, and crab meat and is located next to Cooks Landing. You can come by land or boat.

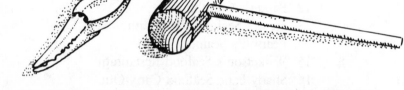

MILFORD HAVEN CRAB HOUSE OF VA.
Gwynn's Island, Virginia
804/725-2140

Business Season: all year

Hours: 5 AM to 5 PM daily

Carry Out Only

Dockage Available: Milford Haven

Crab Cookery: fresh picked crab meat, hot steamed crabs, soft shell crabs, and deviled crab

If you want seafood at its best, I suggest you sample some of the crab cookery prepared by Jerry Jagger and Sandra Forrest at Milford Haven Crab House. Steamed and deviled crabs were my choice. I sat at the water's edge at the lone picnic table and enjoyed the wonderful view while putting away another dozen. I am looking forward to my next visit. Will I see you there?

L. & L. FISH MARKET

Gwynn's Island, Virginia
804/725-5222

Business Season: all year

Hours: Monday through Friday—9 AM to 5 PM, Saturday—8 AM to 5 PM, Sunday—8 AM to 4 PM

Carry Out Only

Dockage Available: Milford Haven

Crab Cookery: crab meat—fresh picked, soft shell crabs, deviled crab, and hot steamed crabs with Baltimore Spice

L. & L. Fish Market is your first stop to the treasures of tiny and beautiful Gwynn's Island, Virginia.

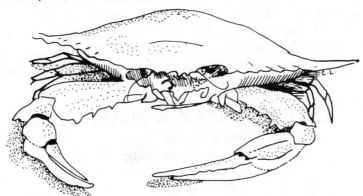

CLIFFORD WINSTEAD'S CRABS

Route 3—Lancaster Road
Irvington, Virginia
804/438-5429

Business Season: June to September

Hours: 8 AM to 7 PM, 7 days

Carry Out Only

Crab Cookery: hot steamed crabs

Mr. Winstead's backyard crabs can be found adjacent to the front gate of the Tide's Inn in downtown Irvington. Just follow the driveway around to the backyard and the precious crabs—YUM.

RAPPAHANNOCK OYSTER COMPANY
Route 672
Kilmarnock, Virginia
804/435-1605

Business Season: all year

Hours: Monday through Friday—10 AM to 6 PM, Saturday and Sunday—8 AM to 6 PM

Carry Out Only

Dockage Available: Indian Creek

Crab Cookery: soft shell crabs, crab meat, live crabs, steamed crabs, crab imperial, crab cakes, crab salad, crab cheese balls, and deviled crabs

If you are driving, Rappahannock Oyster Company is located on Rt. 672, 1 mile past the Indian Creek Yacht Club and if you come by water, stop at daymark #8 on Indian Creek just off the Bay midway between Smith Pt. and Windmill Pt., Grog Island and Pittman's Cove. You can stop at the dock or anchor out at our safe, secure anchorage. Our launch provides on-board delivery for your seafood order.

TAPPAHANNOCK SEAFOOD
Route 17 and 360
at Hoskins Creek Bridge
Tappahannock, Virginia
804/443-2503

Business Season: June to September

Hours: Monday through Friday—10 AM to 6 PM, Saturday—7 AM to 8 PM, closed Sunday

Carry Out Only

Crab Cookery: crabs—hard or soft, steamed or live, and dozen or bushel sales

The northern neck of Virginia is a narrow and picturesque peninsula as beautiful and unspoiled today as when first visited by Capt. John Smith in 1608. Today's visitor can hunt, fish, swim, sail, explore history, or simply relax and enjoy the scenery. If you are going to do all that, you had better include a bushel of crabs from Tappahannock Seafood.

NORTHERN NECK SEAFOOD

Highway 360
Red Hill
Warsaw, Virginia
804/333-3225

Business Season: all year

Hours: 8 AM. to 8 PM daily

Carry Out Only

Crab Cookery: steamed crabs, soft crabs, fresh crab meat, deviled crabs, and crab cakes

Northern Neck Seafood is located between Tappahannock and Warsaw at Red Hill. Mike Hutt is your host for beer, ice, and bait and our favorite food...so don't wait, hurry by for delectable hot steamed crabs.

KEYSER BROTHERS, INC.

Box 280
Lottsburg, Virginia
804/529-6837

Business Season: year round

Hours: closed Sunday, 8 AM to 6 PM daily

Carry Out Only

Dockage Available: Coan Creek, Glebe River

Crab Cookery: live or steamed hard shell crabs

Surrounded by natural waterways and laced with creeks and inlets, the northern neck area of the Chesapeake Bay is of natural and breathtaking beauty. Insert a working crab and oyster house at the water's edge and you have the Keyser Brothers, dealers of crab meat. If you are driving, once in Callao, turn left off of Route 360, turn left again on Route 614, and another left on 627 will bring you to Keyser's.

CAPT. FAUNCE SEAFOOD
Route 2
Montross, Virginia
804/493-8690

Business Season: year round

Hours: 8 AM to 8 PM

Carry Out Only

Crab Cookery: crab meat and hot steamed crabs

Waterman Bill Howeth, purveyor of oysters, crabs, and shrimp and proprietor of Capt. Faunce Seafood, reminisced about his earlier days in Washington and suburban Maryland. He was quick to give praise to his current location in the northern neck of Virginia, a land comprised of three large peninsulas bordered by the Potomac, Rappahannock, and York Rivers and fronted by the majestic Chesapeake Bay. It is a prime spot for a business that enables him to oversee a year-round seafood market.

I was allowed to see Bill's crab operation. With pride, he offered a sample of his mysterious crab seasoning; only with hesitation did he admit me into the room where he prepares this spicy mix. Next, we came to the crab picking room where Bill explained that he was certified to have nine crab pickers. He pointed to the long stainless steel table that filled the tiny room as he spoke. We looked around to see shiny white floors and walls and took note that in one corner a single table was designated for a worker to crack and pack the mounds of crab claws.

Bill took me to a screened rear porch where the crab cooking took place. The large stainless steel vats used only live steam to cook the crabs and Bill assured me his was the best method for preparing them.

Next time you are in Montross, stop at Capt. Faunce Seafood. See Bill and sample some fine seafood. You won't be disappointed.

PETE ALLEN OYSTER
COMPANY AND SEAFOOD
Route 1
Montross, Virginia
804/493-8711

Business Season: year round

Hours: 7 AM to 7 PM (hours extended to 9:30 PM during crab season)

Carry Out Only

Crab Cookery: steamed or live and hard or soft crabs, crab cakes, deviled crab, crab claws by the pound, and oysters

Pete and Lucy Allen depend upon the life in the Chesapeake Bay for their livelihood, which is made by selling crabs and oysters at their roadside market. They share with us their recipe for crab cakes:

Crab Cakes

6 slices bread	3 eggs lightly beaten
½ cup melted butter	¼ cup mayonnaise
2 tbsp. lemon juice	2 tbsp. baking powder
2 tbsp. worcestershire sauce	1 tbsp. McCormick Seafood Seasoning
1½ tsp. salt	shortening
3 lbs. crab meat	

Break bread into fine crumbs. Add the remaining ingredients except crab meat. Mix well, then combine with crab meat. Shape into cakes. Fry in hot shortening or deep fat at 375° for three minutes or until brown. Makes 24 cakes.

WINTER HARBOR SEAFOOD
Route 3
Oak Grove, Virginia
804/224-7779

Business Season: all year

Hours: 8 AM to 9 PM, 7 days

Carry Out Only

Crab Cookery: live and steamed hard crabs and fresh soft crabs

Winter Harbor Seafood is located on Route 3, 1 mile east of Oak Grove. Owned and operated by E. W. Bowie and sons, this market offers general merchandise as well as a unique and fresh approach to the northern neck region's many delights. Try Winter Harbor's hot steamed crabs and you will be delighted too.

PARKER'S CRAB SHORE
1008 Monroe Bay Drive
Colonial Beach, Virginia
804/224-7090

Business Season: March through October

Hours: 8:30 AM to 10 PM

Eat In/Carry Out

Dockage Available: Monroe Bay

Crab Cookery: steamed crabs, crab cakes, soft crab, crab Norfolk, crab salad, and imperial crab

At Parker's Crab Shore, your crabs are prepared in an outdoor crab cooking room just at the water's edge on Monroe Bay. This traditional crab cooking was the method used by founder Clay Parker over 55 years ago. Family members still operate in the same manner today.

STEVE'S SEAFOOD RESTAURANT
Monroe Bay Drive
Colonial Beach, Virginia
804/224-7360

Business Season: year round

Hours: 11 AM to midnight, 7 days

Eat In/Carry Out

Dockage Available: Monroe Bay

Crab Cookery: steamed or live hard crabs, crab soup, crab cakes, and crab meat Norfolk

We travel to Colonial Beach at least once a year and each visit means a stop at Steve's Seafood Restaurant. Steve's has a regular following of Washingtonians that, like us, return because we like the food and the lovely view of Monroe Bay.

PEARSON'S SEAFOOD
610 Colonial Avenue
Colonial Beach, Virginia
804/224-7511

Business Season: April to November

Hours: 9 AM to 6 PM

Carry Out Only

Crab Cookery: live or steamed crabs and soft crabs

Located in town, just a trotline from the waterline, you will find Pearson's Seafood. This market is a convenient stop when visiting Colonial Beach to buy bait, lines, crab nets, or fishing gear. Or, do as we did and try eating their crabs. The crabs were freshly steamed and we drove out of town to the nearby Westmoreland State Park where we found an empty picnic table at the water's edge. There we proceeded to polish off a dozen superbly steamed crabs.

WILKERSON'S SEAFOOD RESTAURANT
Route 205
Colonial Beach, Virginia
804/224-7117
804/224-7118

Business Season: all year

Hours: 11:30 AM to 9 PM, 7 days a week

Dockage Available: Potomac River

Eat In/Carry Out

Crab Cookery: steamed hard crabs, soft shell crabs, crab soup, crab Norfolk, crab newburg, crab imperial, and crab cocktail

Besides good crabs, another asset of Wilkerson's is its panoramic view of the Potomac River. Wilkerson's is a nice family restaurant that is clean and airy and can easily be reached by car or boat.

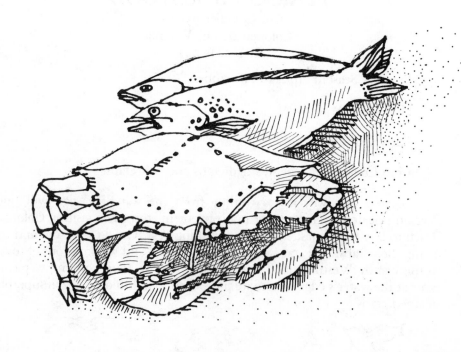

SHADY LANE SEAFOOD CARRY-OUT

Highway 205
Colonial Beach, Virginia
804/224-7878

Business Season: April to November

Hours: 11 AM to 8 PM, 7 days a week

Carry Out Only

Crab Cookery: Maryland and Virginia crabs—live or steamed
with Shady Lane's own special blend of seasoning

Shady Lane's own special blend of seasoning is just one of the treats in
coming to Colonial Beach, "The Playground of the Potomac."

Owner Elgin Nininger, Jr. shares with us his recipe for Crab Louis.

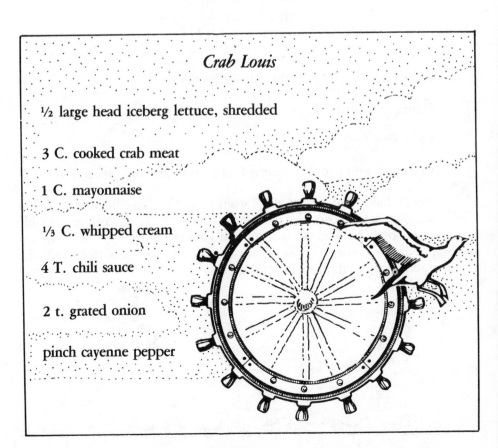

Crab Louis

½ large head iceberg lettuce, shredded

3 C. cooked crab meat

1 C. mayonnaise

⅓ C. whipped cream

4 T. chili sauce

2 t. grated onion

pinch cayenne pepper

ROY'S SEAFOOD
Route 218
King George, Virginia
703/775-2384

Business Season: May to November

Hours: weekdays—9 AM to 8 PM, weekdays—9 AM to 9 PM

Carry Out Only

Crab Cookery: steamed or live hard shell crabs

Roy Fenwick, like his father, has been a waterman all of his life. Today, he applies a lifetime of experience in preparing delicious crabs.

BAREFOOT GREEN'S SEAFOOD
1017 Sophia Street
Fredericksburg, Virginia
703/373-2012

Business Season: April through December

Hours: 8 AM to 7 PM

Carry Out Only

Crab Cookery: live and steamed hard crabs and crab meat

Rumor has it that ''Barefoot'' Green was unbeatable, having never lost a fight. As a local boxer, he earned a reputation for his unquestionable ability to box. The seafood market and convenience store that bears his name today is owned by Joe Bourne who steams crabs that, like the namesake of his establishment, are unbeatable!

NEWTON SEAFOOD
809 White Oak Road
Fredericksburg, Virginia
703/371-0222

Business Season: March to November

Hours: 9 AM to 6 PM

Carry Out Only

Crab Cookery: oysters, steamed crabs, and live crabs

Newton Seafood sells fresh fish daily, and when they are in season, oysters and clams are offered along with steamed crabs and live crabs.

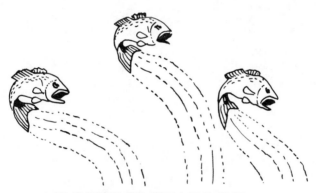

BOURNE SEAFOOD
Route 11, Box 523
Fredericksburg, Virginia
703/373-4637

Business Season: year round

Hours: 7 AM to 7 PM

Carry Out Only

Crab Cookery: soft shell crabs, hot steamed Virginia crabs, crab meat, and oysters

Mr. Bourne's backyard crab market caters to four kinds of people: people who love crabs, people who love crab meat, people who love oysters, and people who love conversation while they make their selection.

Crabbing with Matt on the Galesville Pier.

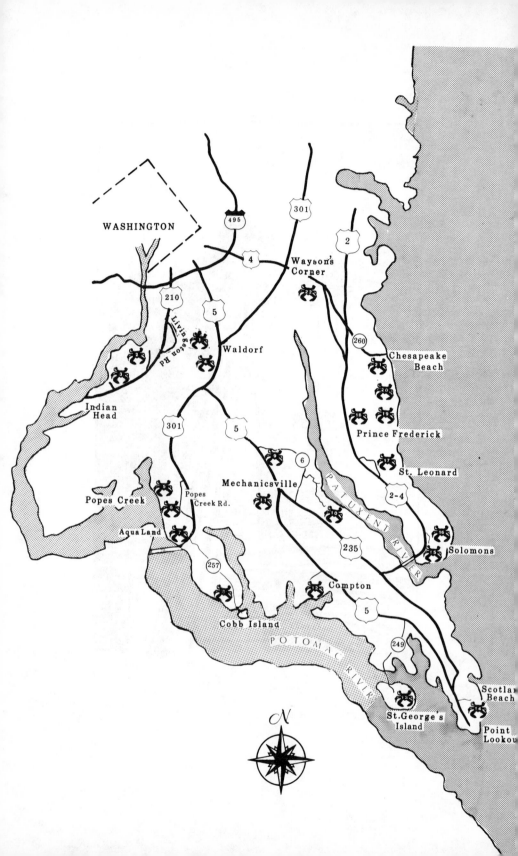

Southern Maryland Crab Houses

1. B & G Tavern
2. Lantern Club
3. Mick's Quail Inn
4. Ted's Seafood Market
5. Robertson's Crab House
6. Popes Creek Pier
7. Mr. Crab's Sombrero
8. Captain John's Seafood Restaurant
9. Copsey's Seafood Restaurant
10. Drift Inn Seafood
11. Seafood Corner Market
12. Harbor View Inn
13. Evan's Crab House
14. Duffy's Tavern
15. Thomas' Crab House
16. Solomons Crab House
17. Tommie's Crab House
18. Ms. Lizzie's Seafood & Carryout
19. Abner's Seaside Crab House
20. Rod 'N' Reel Crab House
21. Tyler's Tackle Shop and Crab House
22. Bradshaw Bros. Crab House

B & G TAVERN
14602 Livingston Road
Accokeek, Maryland
301/292-4188

Business Season: April through October

Hours: 9 AM to 12 PM

Eat In/Carry Out

Crab Cookery: J.O. Seasoning is used to spice steamed Chesapeake Bay crabs; crab feast Wednesday and Friday—7 PM to 11 PM, Sunday—4 PM to 7 PM

It was early November when I discovered the B & G Tavern and was told, "We pride ourselves on Maryland crabs. Please come back in the spring." We did and, to our delight, the Surf Room at the B & G Tavern was just the place to begin the crab season. The tavern was packed and noisy with the sound of folks cracking and eating some of the first crabs of the season.

Owner Mark Scheibert shares the following recipes with us.

Crab Cakes

1 lb. crab meat	2 T. mayonnaise
dash tabasco	2 eggs
1/4 t. salt	1 T. mustard
1/8 t. pepper	1 T. dried parsley

Combine all and mix lightly, roll in cracker crumbs, fry until golden brown in color.

Crab Salad

1/4 t. salt	2 t. mustard
2 t. worcestershire sauce	2 stalks celery, chopped
	1 T. onion, minced
3 heaping T. mayonnaise	1 lb. backfin crab meat

Mix all and serve in lettuce or tomato cups.

LANTERN CLUB

Route 227
Marshall Hall, Maryland
301/283-5438

Business Season: February 1st through December 31st

Hours: Monday through Friday—4 PM to 2 AM, Saturday—11 AM to 2 AM, Sunday—11 AM to midnight

Eat In/Carry Out

Crab Cookery: hot steamed crabs, homemade crab cakes, caters crab feasts, vegetable crab soup, soft crab sandwich, and J.O. Spice

Sonny Tice first sold crabs roadside for 9 years in his steamer truck, a business now operated by his son, Moe. Sonny's steamer truck cooking method continues at the Lantern Club as an unique catering service for your crab feasts. Sonny can produce hot-on-the-spot, up to ten steaming bushels of crabs in 40 minutes in your own backyard or picnic site. Or, you can visit Sonny at his country roadside crab house in downtown Marshall Hall, Maryland. Either way, you are in for a delightful crab eating experience.

175

MICK'S QUAIL INN

63 Glymont Road
Indian Head, Maryland
301/743-3666
301/753-6251

Business Season: April through November

Hours: 11 AM to midnight daily

Eat In/Carry Out

Crab Cookery: all-you-can-eat crab feast on Tuesday, Saturday, and Sunday, by the dozen or bushel anytime

Mick's Quail Inn demonstrates imagination and may possess the most original name for a crab house. Mick's originally earned its unique reputation by preparing feasts that offered many of the game birds found throughout southern Maryland. Today, that same reputation is extended to their crab cookery. They also have a buffet that offers many exciting local seafood flavors.

TED'S SEAFOOD MARKET
Route 301
Waldorf, Maryland
301/645-1646
301/843-2033

Business Season: open 7 days a week all year

Hours: summer hours: 9 AM to 9 PM daily; winter hours: Monday through Thursday—9 AM to 7:30 PM, Friday and Saturday—9 AM to 9 PM, Sunday 10 AM to 7:30 PM

Carry Out Only

Crab Cookery: hot steamed crabs, soft crabs, and crab meat

As one waterman put it, "If you're in the crab business, sooner or later you will meet at Ted's."

Ted's is one of the most popular seafood markets in southern Maryland. It is evident that the Brown family takes great pride in their business of serving people. Regular customers are called each week and advised of the fresh seafood specials available.

It is in this same "spirit of service" that cousin Ray Brown extends his time to the local school systems by teaching students the art of picking steamed hard shell crabs.

Frances' Crab Cakes

1 slightly beaten egg

¼ C. milk

¼ C. mayonnaise

1 t. wet mustard

1 lb. backfin lump crab meat

cracker crumbs as needed

Mix gently ingredients in order given, adding cracker crumbs as needed to form 8 patties. Refrigerate 1 hour. Fry in butter until golden brown.

ROBERTSON'S CRAB HOUSE
Popes Creek Road
Popes Creek, Maryland
301/934-9236

Business Season: open 7 days a week Memorial Day through Labor Day, closed January and February, open weekends only March and April

Hours: Monday through Saturday—11 AM to 9 PM

Eat In/Carry Out

Dockage Available: Potomac River

Crab Cookery: crab feast Monday through Friday, crab cakes, and the "back rub"

Crabs sold for 50 cents a dozen on April 20, 1930. That was the day that Connor Butler started cooking crabs at Popes Creek, Maryland. Popes Creek offered a ferry and train depot and the crab shack stood at the water's edge. Connor prepared crabs for the train and ferry passengers. He would take their orders in the morning and have the hot, spicy crabs ready for the commute home in the evening. The Robertson family purchased the crab shack in the mid-1930's; with the business came Connor Butler.

Joe and Pam Robertson are the proud third generation owners of Robertson's Crab House. Joe tends bar and oversees the crab orders. Pam designed the attractive menus and assists in the kitchen. Connor, still cooking, understands the simple majesty of steamed crabs—prepared with just the right seasoning and cooked with exact timing—he performs a feat which has been perfected in his more than 50 years of crab cooking.

The ferry has since been replaced by the Potomac River Bridge. Only a shell of the railroad depot remains. For many, the shack has become a thriving southern Maryland tradition complete with a pine panelled interior filled with long tables and booths. Vinegar bottles, pleated paper cups of salt and cayenne pepper, along with wooden mallets and paring knives on brown butcher paper are your condiments and tools for good crab eating.

POPES CREEK PIER
Popes Creek Road
Popes Creek, Maryland
301/259-2114

Business Season: year round

Hours: open Tuesday through Thursday—4 PM to 10 PM; Friday and Saturday—11 AM to 11 PM; Sunday—11 AM to 10 PM

Eat In/Carry Out

Dockage Available: Popes Creek Pier, Potomac River

Crab Cookery: crab feast every day except Sunday—all-you-can-eat until supply is gone

The management of Popes Creek Pier (formerly Captain Drink's) takes great pride in the fact that they have regular customers who return every year. Captain Drink's was a favorite of many older Washingtonians who remember the era of the slot machines, a tradition that ended in the late 1960's. It was rumored that southern Maryland had as many slot machines as Las Vegas. Perhaps it's their memories of the good times when they enjoyed crab feasts with beer by taking a jaunt away from the city that keeps them coming back. Better still, it could be their anticipation of more good times in the future in Popes Creek.

Fried Hard Crab

Using a large steamed crab (top shell, gills, and stomach have been removed and it has been washed very clean), stuff with lump crab meat, dip in seasoned batter, and fry to a golden brown.

MR. CRAB'S SOMBRERO
Aqualand at the Bridge
Route 301
Newburg, Maryland
301/259-4477

Business Season: all year

Hours: 11 AM to 10 PM, 7 days a week

Eat In/Carry Out

Dockage Available: Potomac River

Crab Cookery: ''Anyone can cook crabs, but nobody can season and steam them the way Dennis Conner can—his specialty for well over 30 years.''

The menu from Mr. Crab's Sombrero greets you with:

"BIENVENIDO! Welcome to the exciting and romantic place of fine seafood and Mexican food where you will enjoy the fresh taste of Maryland crabs, seafood and the fine foods of Mexican cuisine that started with the Aztec and Mayan cultures.

Sit back, relax, order your favorite drink, enjoy the serenity of the Potomac River and allow us the pleasure of making your dining an unforgetable experience.''

This says it all about Mr. Crab's Sombrero except that you'll want to go back as often as you can.

CAPTAIN JOHN'S SEAFOOD RESTAURANT
Route 254
Cobb Island, Maryland
301/259-2315

Business Season: open year round

Hours: 7:30 AM to 11 PM, 7 days a week

Eat In/Carry Out

Dockage Available: Neal Sound and Potomac River

Crab Cookery: crab cakes, deviled crab, crab soup, and hot steamed crabs

Captain John's Seafood Restaurant is located adjacent to the Cobb Island Bridge. Captain John's welcomes you at the entrance with a daily listing of prices and crab specials.

Two large rooms are available for crab eating, one offers a spacious bar area and T.V. while the other affords a beautiful view of marina and harbor traffic. The back room, used as a carry out, features oysters, fresh fish, and, of course, crabs.

Captain John's is an excellent restaurant, featuring fine food and a comfortable atmosphere.

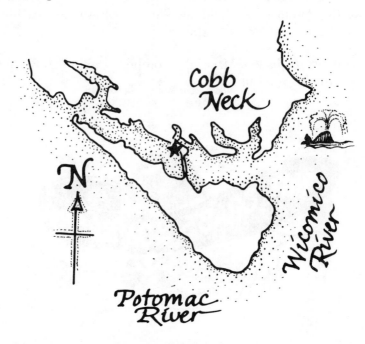

COPSEY'S SEAFOOD RESTAURANT
Route 5
Mechanicsville, Maryland
301/884-4235 • 301/884-8250

Business Season: year round

Hours: 10 AM to 10 PM, 7 days a week

Eat In/Carry Out

Crab Cookery: steamed crabs, deviled crab, crab cake, soft crab, and imperial crab

Clements W. Copsey and sons are the owners of this wayside crab house, as the sign over the center door proudly states.

On the left of the entrance is the traditional crab room with 12 long tables. It is kept warm in the winter by a solitary wood stove.

A small center room reveals a blackboard that displays the menu. The day's listings include crab cakes, deviled crabs and hot steamed Louisiana crabs. A view of the tiny kitchen through a small window and the sweet smell of crab cookery lets us know we are in for good eating.

Customers can look over a small array of basic essentials for sale while waiting for their crab orders. A seafood case is filled with king crab legs, crab cakes, and crab imperial. Old Bay Seasoning, vinegar and a bottle of Jack Daniels on a wall shelf are part of the decor.

At the small cash register there is a sign which tells us we are in the "Home of the 1980 World's Oyster Shucking Champion (men's division), Wayne Copsey, Jr." Congratulations, Wayne!

DRIFT INN SEAFOOD
Drift Inn Road
Oraville, Maryland
301/884-3470

Business Season: all year

Hours: Saturday, and Sunday—1 PM until supply is gone

Eat In/Carry Out

Dockage Available: Patuxent River

Crab Cookery: live or steamed hard crabs, fresh oysters, crab cakes, and soft shell crab sandwiches

Drift Inn Seafood has been serving delicious hot steamed hard shell crabs for over 30 years. During that time, Leonard Copsey has earned the respect of local crab lovers.

It was opened in 1953 and still sells crabs in the summer and oysters in the winter. The Copsey family takes pride in their cooked crabs, served, as it always has been, by one of Mr. Copsey's daughters or grandchildren.

SEAFOOD CORNER MARKET
Route 5
Mechanicsville, Maryland
301/884-5251

Business Season: local crabs are served through December

Hours: Tuesday, Wednesday, and Thursday—11 AM to 7 PM; Friday and Saturday—10 AM to 8 PM; Sunday—10 AM to 5 PM; closed Monday

Carry Out Only

Crab Cookery: Bay crabs—live or steamed, hard or soft, crab cakes, deviled crab, and caters crab feasts

Since 1978, Paul Thompson has been the owner of the Seafood Corner Market. Appropriately named, it is located on the corner next to Fitzgerald's Bar and Liquor Store in Mechanicsville. The Corner Market is a small place with a great taste in Paul Thompson's crab cookery.

HARBOR VIEW INN
Route 243
Compton, Maryland
301/475-9432

Business Season: all year

Hours: weekdays—11 AM to 12 PM, Friday and Saturday—11 AM to 12 PM

Eat In/Carry Out

Dockage Available: Combs Creek, Breton Bay

Crab Cookery: J.O. Spice and steamed crabs

Helen's Hideaway at the Harbor View Inn has country music, pool tables and turkey shoots. It also has a downstairs crab feast room where your host, Helen Pilkerton, offers delicious hard shell crabs as well as a beautiful view from her windows of Combs Creek, which is a short curve of land beyond beautiful Breton Bay.

EVAN'S CRAB HOUSE
St. George's Island, Maryland
301/994-2299

Business Season: all year

Hours: Tuesday through Friday—4 PM to 11 PM, Saturday and Sunday—noon to 11 PM, closed Monday

Eat In / Carry Out

Dockage Available: St. George's Creek

Crab Cookery: soft shell crab sandwiches, steamed hard crabs, crab cakes, and crab imperial

Horseshoes, hotdogs, and hydroplanes first attracted me to St. George's Island. Camping with family and friends on Piney Point, pitching horseshoes under the lights at downtown Swann's Pier, and watching the boat races on St. George's Creek are but a few of the activities that brought me to this unique area.

Hard shell crabs from Evan's Crab House keep me coming back. Evan's sits in the middle of this tiny, narrow island, surrounded by tall sheltering pines. Robert "Bugsy" Evans opened his southern Maryland eatery in 1963, and since that time, his restaurant has become one of the most outstanding and well-known crab houses in the state.

DUFFY'S TAVERN
Scotland Beach
Scotland, Maryland 301/872-4001

Business Season: April 15th to November 15th

Hours: 8 AM to 12 PM, 7 days a week

Eat In/Carry Out

Dockage Available: Chesapeake Bay

Crab Cookery: steamed crabs, crab soup, and cornbread

Built around 1900, Duffy's Tavern was once a port, post office, bowling alley, and general store; it is now a tavern complete with time-worn pine panelling, pot belly stove, and a splendid view of the Bay. Below is one of Mrs. Duffy's favorite and delicious down-home recipes.

Duffy's Crab Soup

In a large soup pot, put 2 lbs. chuck beef with one ham bone or couple ham hocks. Cover with water and cook about 2 hours or until meat is tender. Chop meat and put back in pot with the bone. Add 1 lb. frozen mixed vegetables or use same amount of fresh peas, carrots, string beans, lima beans, 1 large onion, a large green pepper, 1 turnip if available. Add ½ cup celery all chopped fine, 1 head cabbage shredded but not too fine, 6 medium potatoes chopped small. Add 1 large can tomato sauce or fresh tomato chopped. Cover all with generous amount of water and cook all together 2 or 3 hours or until vegetables are done. The longer the soup simmers, the better the flavor. Make sure you keep generous amount of water. Last hour of cooking, add 1 dozen crab bodies that have been cleaned and cut in half. Add legs and 1 tsp. Old Bay, 2 Tbs. cooking sherry, salt and pepper to taste, ¼ tsp. cayenne pepper. (You can use your own favorite recipe for vegetable soup.) At last hour of cooking, add crabs, Old Bay, salt and pepper, sherry, and cayenne pepper.

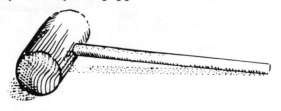

THOMAS' CRAB HOUSE
Main Street
Solomons, Maryland
301/326-3291

Business Season: March to December

Hours: sunrise to dark

Carry Out Only

Crab Cookery: live, hard, and soft crabs

How many times have we heard, "If I had known they sold crabs there, I would have brought some home?" When visiting Solomons Island, a small, beautiful place, stop by Thomas' Crab House. Shirley and Charles Thomas have been supplying the public with daily bushel sales of live hard crabs for over 20 years. Now you know they sell crabs, bring some home.

SOLOMONS CRAB HOUSE
Route 2/4
Solomons, Maryland
301/326-2800

Business Season: year round

Hours: 11 AM to 10 PM, 7 days a week

Eat In/Carry Out

Crab Cookery: crab cakes, soft shell crabs, crab sandwich, crab claws, and hot 'n' spicy Maryland steamed crabs

When asked how he ventured into the crab business, Bill Gottleid, the owner of Solomons Crab House, replied:

"I loved Solomons from the moment I first visited here. I loved the natural harbor. I loved the smell of the salt air, the view, and the crabs. I was disappointed that Solomons had no place to sit and enjoy hot steamed crabs. So, when the old firehouse went up for sale, I decided to take a chance. I was a foreman pipefitter for 25 years and I was ready to make a move. With the help of my family, we completely remodeled the building and now have a 150 seat restaurant; we plan to double the seating by summer.

Our crab supply is supported by the local watermen. When the crabs are running, we catch our own and serve them from right out of the water. We also have professional crab pickers who daily pick the crab meat that we use in our crab cakes. They are 100-percent meat, no filler is used."

You, too, will love the old firehouse crabs and the natural harbor view, the sea air, and the tiny, peaceful island.

TOMMIE'S CRAB HOUSE
Route 765
St. Leonard, Maryland
301/586-9883

Business Season: year round

Hours: 9 AM to 9 PM, 7 days a week

Carry Out Only

Crab Cookery: live and steamed crabs, hard and soft crabs

Tommie's Crab House is a roadside seafood market that specializes in fresh, local seafood. T.C. Wood has been the proprietor of Tommie's for 30 years. We suggest you try his delightful crabs.

MS. LIZZIE'S SEAFOOD & CARRYOUT
Route 4
Prince Frederick, Maryland
301/535-5356

Business Season: all year

Hours: Monday through Friday—6 AM to 9 PM, Saturday—10 AM to 10 PM, and Sunday—10 AM to 8 PM

Carry Out Only

Crab Cookery: steamed hard crabs, crab cakes, crab meat, and caters to crab feasts

The word is out about Ms. Lizzie's steamed crabs and you will want to include her delicious eatery on your crab list.
Ms. Lizzie's can be found in the Weem's Realty Building.

ABNER'S SEASIDE CRAB HOUSE
Harbor Road
Chesapeake Beach, Maryland
301/257-3689

Business Season: April through mid-December

Hours: Sunday through Thursday—11 AM to 10 PM, Friday and Saturday—11 AM to 11 PM

Eat In/Carry Out

Dockage Available: Fishing Creek, Chesapeake Bay

Crab Cookery: crab soup, "Crabner's Stew," fried hard crabs, and hot steamed crabs

A slice of the waterman's life is available at Abner's Seaside Crab House. Abner's is complete with a harbor road at the front door and a fishing creek at the back.

The mainstay of this crab spot is its reputation for preparing good steamed crabs season after season. It's best for you to call ahead for feast reservations or catering.

Louise's Crab Cakes

1 lb. can crab meat

¼ C. mayonnaise

½ C. bread crumbs

1 t. Old Bay Seasoning

¼ t. salt

¼ t. pepper

1 t. parsley flakes

1 egg

Remove all cartilage from crab meat. In a bowl, mix bread crumbs, egg, mayonnaise and seasonings. Add crab meat and mix gently. Shape into six cakes. Cook cakes in enough fat to prevent sticking until browned or cakes can be deep fried at 350 degrees for 2 to 3 minutes until browned.

ROD 'N' REEL CRAB HOUSE

Route 261
Chesapeake Beach, Maryland
301/257-6227

Business Season: July to Labor Day

Hours: 10 AM to 7 PM

Carry Out Only

Dockage Available: Fishing Creek, Chesapeake Bay

Crab Cookery: steamed crabs or live crabs

Jack Abbott's original location was at the end of the pier that extended out into the Bay off the Rod 'n' Reel Club in Chesapeake Beach. During the late 1950's, Hurricane Hazel, in her path, took everything. Jack relocated to the far end of the parking lot. Today, his Fishing Creek location provides a screened-in porch where you can view the active water life on the creek while waiting for your hot, tasty crabs.

TYLER'S TACKLE SHOP & CRAB HOUSE

Route 261
Chesapeake Beach, Maryland
301/257-6610

Business Season: May to November

Hours: weekdays—6 AM to 6 PM, Saturday and Sunday—5 AM to 6 PM

Carry Out Only

Crab Cookery: live or steamed crabs and Old Bay Seasoning

Calvin Tyler sells tackle on the tidewater. The Tackle Shop is in a separate building from the crab house, but both overlook the Bay at Chesapeake Beach, Maryland. Tyler's steamed crabs are cooked to order so they are hot and fresh for you to eat. Just outside the front door, a solitary picnic table is provided for those who want a sample taste before the trip home.

BRADSHAW BROS. CRAB HOUSE

Wayson's Corner
Lothian, Maryland
301/741-9006

Business Season: open 7 days a week beginning April 1st and ending December 31st

Hours: Monday through Friday—2 PM to 10 PM, Saturday and Sunday—12 PM to 11 PM

Eat In/Carry Out

Crab Cookery: hot steamed crabs, crab cakes, and crab stew

Bingo, Bar-B-Q and Bradshaw's crabs are the three main businesses in this tiny road-stop town. Across from the bingo halls, sits Duffy's III and, around in the side parking lot, is Bradshaw Bros. Crab House.

Walking by the crab house, I noticed a small sign taped to the outdoor screen window. It read: "CRAB STEW WITH POTATOES AND DUMPLINGS—95 CENTS PT." Who could resist?

No fooling, Edward and Leslie Bradshaw have been serving Bay crabs since April Fool's Day, 1973. With a little persuasion, the Bradshaw brothers agreed to share the following recipe for their special crab cakes:

Bradshaw Bros. Crab Cakes

1 lb. crab meat	1 t. parsley flakes
bread crumbs or 2 slices of bread	mustard
Old Bay Seasoning	1 T. mayonnaise

In a round bowl, combine the crab meat and the bread crumbs, adding the mayonnaise and a little pinch of mustard. While mixing together, add the parsley flakes and a pinch of Old Bay Seasoning, then make into patties for the crab cakes. Makes about 8.

Robert Marshall, Sr. has room to steam ten
bushels of crabs on his crab truck.

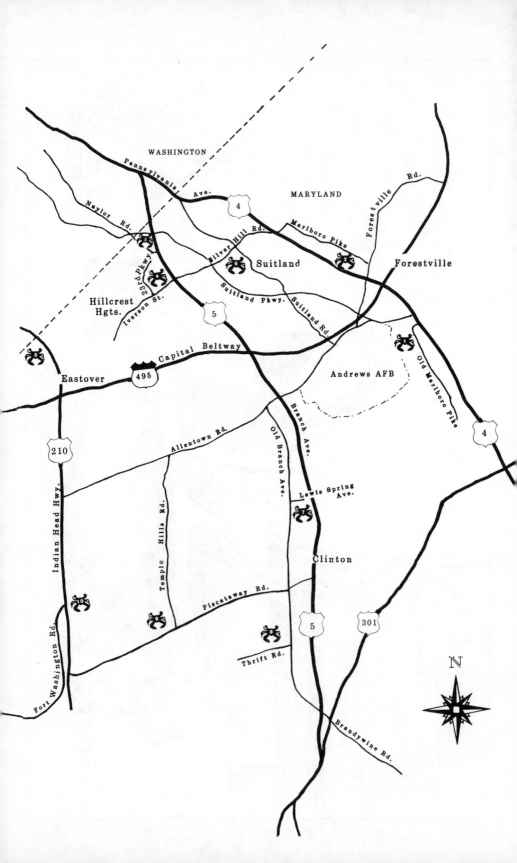

Washington Crab Houses

SOUTHEAST SECTION

1. Cap'n Jim's
2. Crab Line
3. Yesterday's
4. Crabs on Wheels
5. The Fish Mart
6. Crab King
7. Sam's Crab House
8. Gena's Seafood
9. Gena's Seafood
10. Marshall's Crab Truck

CAP'N JIM'S
9207 Old Marlboro Pike
Upper Marlboro, Maryland
301/599-1919

Business Season: 1st of April to 3rd Sunday in September

Hours: Tuesday through Friday—3 PM to 9:30 PM, Saturday and Sunday—12 noon to 9:30 PM, closed Mondays

Carry Out Only

Crab Cookery: crab meat, soft shells, steamed shrimp, and hot steamed crabs

Jim's is located on the Old Marlboro Pike, now just a parallel road to state Route 4 or Pennsylvania Avenue extended. When Cap'n Jim is steaming crabs, he turns on the outside lights which are the eyes of the crab he has painted on the crab house wall. You can see them sparkling from the highway. Don't pass by. You are in for a treat.

An original style crab cookery that blends cayenne pepper and salt makes Cap'n Jim's crabs some of the best in the state.

These original hot steamed crabs have been a Washington area favorite since 1962 and can be found by taking Beltway exit 11A south, turn right at the third traffic light, look for signs...the eyes have it.

CRAB LINE
7607 Marlboro Pike
Forestville, Maryland
301/735-5600

Business Season: year round

Hours: Monday through Thursday—11 AM to 10 PM, Friday and Saturday—11 AM to 11 PM, Sunday—10 AM to 9 PM

Eat In/Carry Out

Crab Cookery: crab cakes, crab soup, and hot steamed crabs

Joe King began his crab business in the late 1960's and his simple approach is his trademark. "Our crabs are steamed in a pot with ½ inch of water with our special spice mix added." You will want to sample, so give Joe a call or plan to come to one of the crab feasts held on Tuesday and Wednesday. You will be more than satisfied.

YESTERDAY'S
3330 Naylor Road
Temple Hills, Maryland
301/894-7764 or 894-5455

Business Season: year round

Hours: 11 AM to 1 AM

Eat In/Carry Out

Crab Cookery: hot steamed crabs

You will want to sample the crabs prepared by Yesterday's using Mary's hot 'n' spicy recipe today...don't wait until tomorrow.

CRABS ON WHEELS
23rd Parkway
Hillcrest Heights, Maryland
301/994-0400

Business Season: March to December

Hours: Tuesday through Saturday and holidays—2 AM to 11 PM

Carry Out Only: crab truck

Crab Cookery: hard, soft, live, and steamed crabs

Vernon and Ida Thompson have been selling crabs in the Hillcrest Heights area for the past 10 years. Their colorfully painted truck, "Crabs on Wheels," occupies a space in the parking lot of Murphy's Five and Dime. Crabs on Wheels is equipped to steam up to six bushels of fresh crabs that are brought in daily from the Thompson's St. George's Island home.

THE FISH MART
5121 Indian Head Highway
Oxon Hill, Maryland
301/839-5858

Business Season: all year

Hours: 10 AM to 9 PM

Carry Out Only

Crab Cookery: crab cakes and hot steamed crabs

This convenient carry out is located just over the District Line in Prince Georges County. You may want to visit The Fish Mart at "Eastover's Wharf" for Maryland and Virginia crabs in the summer and North Carolina and Georgia crabs in the winter. Crabs prepared at The Fish Mart are carefully cooked in a homemade seasoning and are ready to eat and hard to beat.

CRAB KING
4931 Suitland Road
Suitland, Maryland
301/736-7205

Business Season: all year

Hours: Monday thorugh Saturday—11 AM to 9:30 PM,
Sundays—1:30 PM to 6 PM

Carry Out Only

Crab Cookery: live crabs, hot spiced crabs, and homemade crab
cakes

The following short poem by Irma Wedding, the owner of the Crab
King, expresses a view that we share:

Crabs cooked at CRAB KING are really a delight.

You can eat them in the morning and all through the night.

Never have to worry about ever getting fat.

Just buy a bag and try them and that will settle that.

SAM'S CRAB HOUSE
7911 Lewis Spring Avenue
Clinton, Maryland
301/868-4373

Business Season: year round

Hours: Tuesday through Thursday—4 PM to 2 AM, Friday
through Sunday—noon to 2 AM, closed Mondays

Eat In/Carry Out

Crab Cookery: hot steamed crabs

During the week at Sam's Crab House, music is provided by a disc
jockey who spins—but for the crab lover, it's he who wins. Sam's crabs are
cooked to perfection at his country crab house in Clinton.

GENA'S SEAFOOD
10007 Brandywine Road
Clinton, Maryland
301/868-5681

Business Season: open all year except Thanksgiving Day

Hours: Monday through Saturday—11 AM to 11 PM,
Sunday—noon to 10 PM

Eat In/Carry Out

Crab Cookery: steamed crabs, soft crabs, crab cakes, live crabs,
sales by the dozen or bushel, crab soup, and shrimp stuffed
with crab meat

In July 1968, Gene and Nancy Tolson took what was once a one car
garage, installed 11 crab steamers, and turned the lubrication bay into a ten
table crab house.
A good crab house is one that produces delicious steamed crabs time
after time. Gene and Nancy do just that.

GENA'S SEAFOOD
9717 Temple Hills Road
Clinton, Maryland
301/856-1450

Business Season: all year

Hours: 10 AM to 9 PM daily

Carry Out Only

Crab Cookery: hard crabs—live or steamed, soft crabs, and crab
meat

Visit Gena's fresh seafood market. The carry out is located on the
corner of Temple Hills Road and Piscataway Road. A wide variety of seafood
is available fresh daily. This day's listing included croaker, spot, blues,
perch, sea trout, cat fish, butter fish, flounder, rock fish, and, of course,
crabs—live or steamed, by the dozen or by the bushel—delicious!

MARSHALL'S CRAB TRUCK
Indian Head Highway and
Fort Washington Road
Fort Washington, Maryland

Business Season: March 15th to Christmas Eve

Hours: noon to dark

Carry Out Only: crab truck

Crab Cookery: live or spiced steamed crabs

Robert Marshall, Jr. and Sr. operate this crab truck. They first revamped the camper and now have a truck with refrigeration and room to steam ten bushels of crabs.

Marshall's Crab Truck can be found 4 miles south of the Beltway off Indian Head Highway and Fort Washington Drive in Fort Washington, Maryland. You may want to try them.

Matt's Deviled Crab

1 pound crab meat, fresh picked
2 tablespoons chopped onion
3 tablespoons butter
2 tablespoons flour
¾ cup milk
½ teaspoon salt
Dash pepper
½ teaspoon powdered mustard
1 teaspoon Worcestershire sauce
½ teaspoon sage
1½ teaspoon thyme
Dash cayenne pepper
1 tablespoon lemon juice
1 egg, beaten
1 tablespoon chopped parsley
1 tablespoon butter
¼ cup dry bread crumbs

Remove any shell or cartilage from crab meat. Cook onion in butter until tender. Blend in flour. Add milk gradually and cook until thick, stirring constantly. Add seasonings and lemon juice. Stir a little of the hot sauce into egg; add to remaining sauce, stirring constantly. Add parsley and crab meat. Place in 6 well-greased, individual shells or 5-ounce custard cups. Combine butter and crumbs; sprinkle over top of each shell. Bake in a moderate oven, 350° F., for 30 minutes or until brown. Serves 6.

"I'm hot tonight."

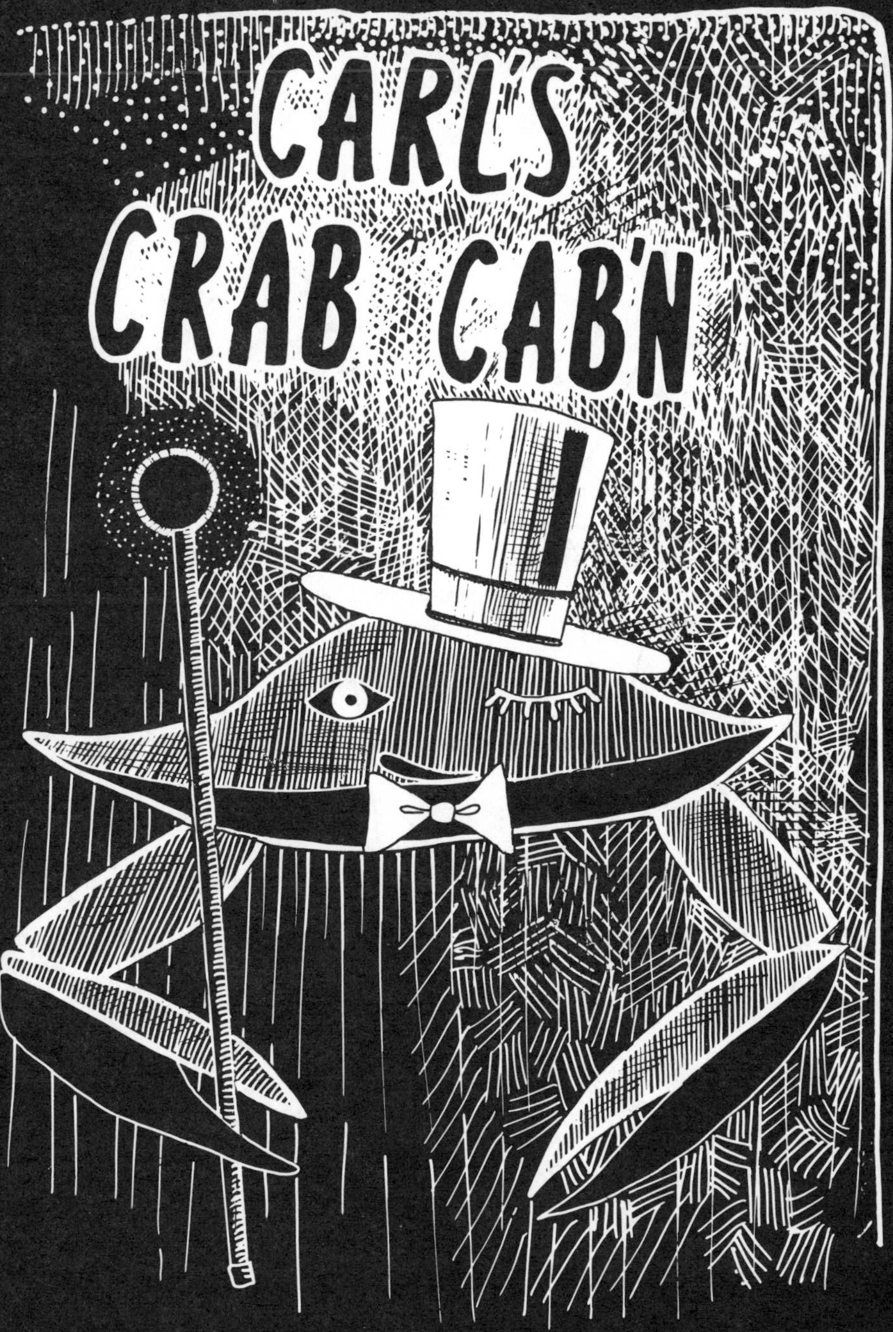
CARL'S
CRAB CAB'N

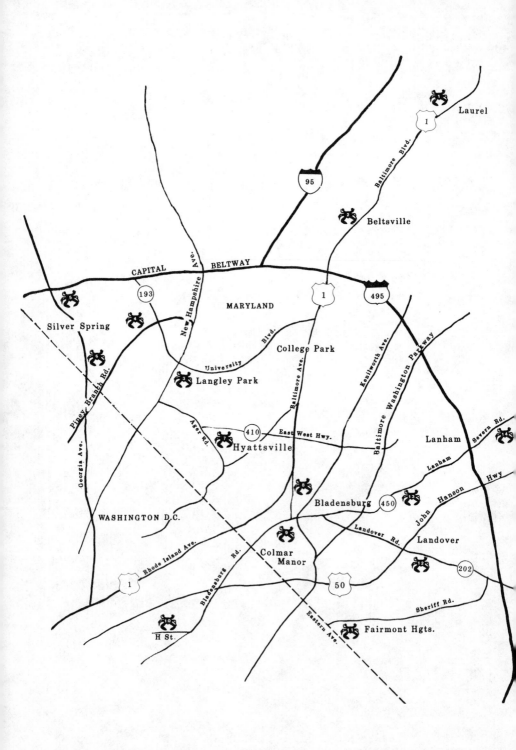

Washington Crab Houses

NORTHEAST SECTION

1. Bottom of the Bay Seafood
2. House of Crabs
3. Carl's Crab Cab'n
4. Chesapeake Crab House
5. Imperial Crab and Seafood
6. Captain White's Seafood Restaurant
7. Crab Pot
8. Crossroads Crab House
9. Ernie's Original Crab House
10. Melvin's Crab House
11. Melvin's Crab House
12. Jimmy's Crab House
13. Pop's Seafood, Inc.
14. Goodluck Seafood

BOTTOM OF THE BAY SEAFOOD
9590 North Laurel Road
Laurel, Maryland
301/498-1040

Business Season: 7 days a week

Hours: noon to 10 PM

Eat In/Carry Out

Crab Cookery: hot steamed crabs

Bottom of the Bay Seafood can be found midway between Washington and Baltimore. My last experience at the Bottom of the Bay topped previous ones. My favorite dishes, crab cakes, crab soup, and hot steamed crabs, were all available and all prepared with a delicious flair.

HOUSE OF CRABS
10620 Baltimore Blvd.
Beltsville, Maryland
301/937-5727

Business Season: all year

Hours: weekdays—3 PM to 10 PM, weekends—1 PM to 11 PM

Carry Out Only

Crab Cookery: hot steamed crabs

Long a legend with locals and visitors alike, the House of Crabs is a nice place to stop and pick-up a dozen crabs to carry home.

Joe Bello and family are proud to serve Maryland crabs seasoned with J.O. spice using the vinegar and water steaming method. You will enjoy eating these tasty crabs.

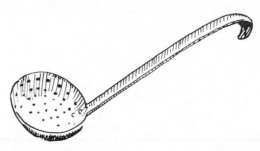

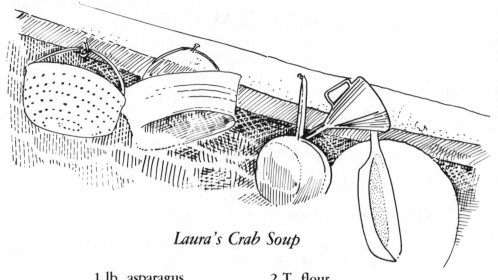

Laura's Crab Soup

1 lb. asparagus	2 T. flour
2 cloves garlic	1 lb. crab meat
2 T. butter	1 c. half and half

Cook asparagus with garlic in boiling salted water to cover. When tender, puree vegetables, reserving the cooking liquid. Melt butter in soup pot. Stir in flour and cook until golden, stirring all the while. Stir in asparagus and the cooking liquid. The mixture should be the consistency of thick cream. Add water or chicken stock if thinning is needed. Add crab meat and cook, stirring for about 12 minutes. Stir in cream after the fire is out; correct seasoning to taste and serve hot.

CARL'S CRAB CAB'N
7643 New Hampshire Avenue
Langley Park, Maryland
301/434-8840

Business Season: year round

Hours: 7 days a week from 11 AM to 11 PM

Carry Out Only

Crab Cookery: steamed crabs—"I'm hot tonight."

Carl Jones opened his Langley Park location in 1972. Today, Carl's "top hat crabs" are his specialty.

CHESAPEAKE CRAB HOUSE
8214 Piney Branch Road
Silver Spring, Maryland
301/589-9868

Business Season: year round

Hours: Monday through Saturday—noon to 10:30 PM
and Sunday—noon to 10 PM

Eat In/Carry Out

Crab Cookery: hot steamed crabs, crab soup, crab
meat cocktail, and crab salad

Want to take your tourist-season guests on a food tour of Washington?
Then begin with the Chesapeake Crab House. Be it a dozen to go or a dozen
to stay, your crab eating time is good, we say.

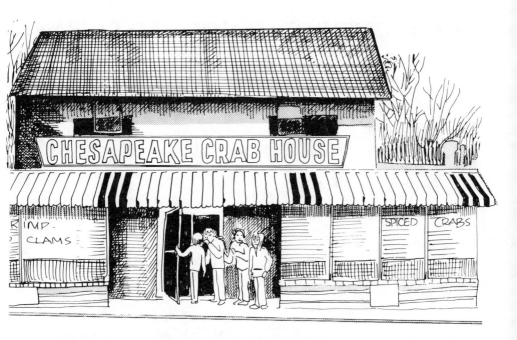

IMPERIAL CRAB AND SEAFOOD
9429 Georgia Avenue
Silver Spring, Maryland
301/589-CRAB

Business Season: all year round

Hours: weekdays—4 PM to 10 PM, Friday and Saturday—4 PM to 11 PM

Eat In/Carry Out

Crab Cookery: crab cakes, crab salad, soft shell crab, crab soup, and hot steamed crabs

The Imperial Crab is located just off the Capitol Beltway (Georgia Avenue exit). Walter Kim, Imperial Crab's host, has earned a reputation for serving quality steamed crabs. In order to sample Mr. Kim's precious crabs, plan to visit the crab feast held nightly.

CAPTAIN WHITE'S SEAFOOD RESTAURANT
8123 Georgia Avenue
Silver Spring, Maryland
301/589-6868

Business Season: all year

Hours: Monday through Thursday—11 AM to 1:30 AM, Friday and Saturday—11 AM to 2:30 AM, Sunday—1 PM to 1:30 AM

Eat In/Carry Out

Crab Cookery: Maryland crabs steamed with J.O. Seasoning

This warm, friendly neighborhood place continues to improve under the ownership of Joe Fabian. Along with good steamed crabs, Joe presents live entertainment on Thursday, Friday, and Saturday evenings.

CRAB FEAST EVERYDAY

CRAB POT
6565 Ager Road
Hyattsville, Maryland
301/422-2323

Business Season: all year

Hours: Monday through Friday—11 AM to 10 PM, Saturday—noon to 11 PM, Sunday—2 PM to 8 PM

Carry Out Only

Crab Cookery: Bay crabs in the summer and Texas crabs in the winter

The Crab Pot is located in the Green Meadows Shopping Center. This carry out provides two picnic tables for those who want immediate satisfaction in good crab eating.

CROSSROADS CRAB HOUSE
4103 Baltimore Avenue
Bladensburg, Maryland
301/927-2332
301/927-5900

Business Season: all year

Hours: 7 days a week from 11 AM to 11 PM

Eat In/Carry Out

Crab Cookery: indoor and outdoor crab catering. . . hot steamed crabs

Top name country and western performers appear nightly at this Peace Cross crab house. A favorite spot since 1959, Crossroads Crab House is now open to serve you at their back alley restaurant and complete carry out crab counter.

ERNIE'S ORIGINAL CRAB HOUSE
4221 Bladensburg Road
Colmar Manor, Maryland
301/779-3013

Business Season: March 1st to December 15th

Hours: noon to 11 PM, 7 days a week

Eat In/Carry Out

Crab Cookery: hot steamed crabs

"Back by popular demand." This Ernie's location is really a treat, enjoy your crabs ready to eat.

Baked Crab Meat in Shells

1 pound crab meat

½ cup chopped spring onion

¼ cup melted butter

2 tablespoons flour

½ cup milk

½ cup tomato sauce

½ teaspoon salt

Dash pepper

¼ cup grated swiss cheese

½ cup soft bread crumbs

Remove any shell or cartilage from crab meat. Cook onion in butter until tender. Blend in flour. Add milk gradually and cook until thick, stirring constantly. Add tomato sauce, seasonings, and crab meat. Place in 6 well-greased, individual shells. Combine cheese and crumbs; sprinkle over top of each shell. Bake in a moderate oven, 350° F., for 20 to 25 minutes or until brown. Serves. 6.

MELVIN'S CRAB HOUSE

644 H Street, N.E.
Washington, D.C.
202/581-1111

711 Eastern Avenue
Fairmont Heights, Maryland
301/322-2267

Business Season: all year

Hours: 12 AM to 12 PM daily

Carry Out Only

Crab Cookery: hot steamed crabs

Melvin's Capitol Hill Crab House (H Street location) is a popular inner city crab eatery that produces hot and heavy crabs time after time. So, now is the time to get in line for crabs at Melvin's.

Melvin Robert's Crab House (Fairmont Heights location) is between two communities (Deanwood in the District of Columbia and Fairmont Heights in Maryland) and so offers a blend of rural Maryland and urban Washington to balance with the sweet blend of herbs and spices of Melvin's crab cookery.

JIMMY'S CRAB HOUSE
7421 Landover Road
Landover, Maryland 20785
301/773-5615
301/773-5616

Business Season: year round

Hours: 8 AM to 2 PM daily

Eat In / Carry Out

Crab Cookery: crabs from Louisiana steamed with J.O.
Seasoning, crab feast in July

Jimmy's Crab House, with its Capital Center location, has been a Prince Georges County favorite for many years. Jimmy's specializes in steamed crabs and steamed shrimp.

POP'S SEAFOOD, INC.
7437 Annapolis Road
Landover Hills, Maryland
301/459-4141

Business Season: all year

Hours: Monday through Thursday—11 AM to 9 PM, Friday and Saturday—11 AM to 10 PM, Sunday—11 AM to 7 PM

Carry Out Only

Crab Cookery: steamed hard crabs medium, large, jumbo, male, female, by the dozen, by the bushel, and caters to onsite crab feast

Joe Berry and Dave Watts say:

Our aim is to provide you with the finest available Blue Crabs. Local Chesapeake Bay Crabs, the World's Finest, are our first priority, supplemented by other markets when local supplies diminish. Crabs are moderately spiced with Baltimore's own 'J.O.' brand seasoning. Extra spice, black pepper style and other seasonings are available on request, and at no extra charge. You are welcome to call ahead for your order—it will be ready when you arrive. Crabs are sold at dozen and bushel prices, and discounts are usually available on quantity orders, depending on market supply. We fish our own crab pots. The catch of the Bay today is your delight tonight."
We say, "Try their crabs."

GOODLUCK SEAFOOD

9035 Lanham Severn Road
Lanham, Maryland
301/459-4500

Business Season: all year

Hours: 10 AM to 10 PM, 7 days a week

Carry Out Only

Crab Cookery: crabs—by the dozen or bushel, male or female, live or cooked, and hot or cold; crab meat; seafood spices and breading; crab mallets; soft shell crabs; frozen (live in season) and caters crab and shrimp feasts

The local newspapers praise this eatery and a T.V. feature will attest to the crabs prepared at Goodluck Seafood, located just off the beltway on Lanham Severn Road, Lanham, Maryland. Don't take the media's word though, try Goodluck yourself.

Scrambled Eggs and Crab

1 pound crab meat

¼ cup chopped bacon

¼ cup chopped onion

4 eggs, beaten

¼ cup milk

¾ teaspoon salt

6 teaspoons fresh chopped basil

Dash pepper

Toast points

Remove any shell or cartilage from crab meat. Fry bacon until lightly brown. Add onion and cook until tender. Combine eggs, milk, seasonings, and crab meat. Add to onion mixture and cook until eggs are firm, stirring occasionally. Serve on toast points. Sprinkle fresh basil on top. Serves 6.

You may get a bang out of Mr. Morgan's "firecracker crabs."

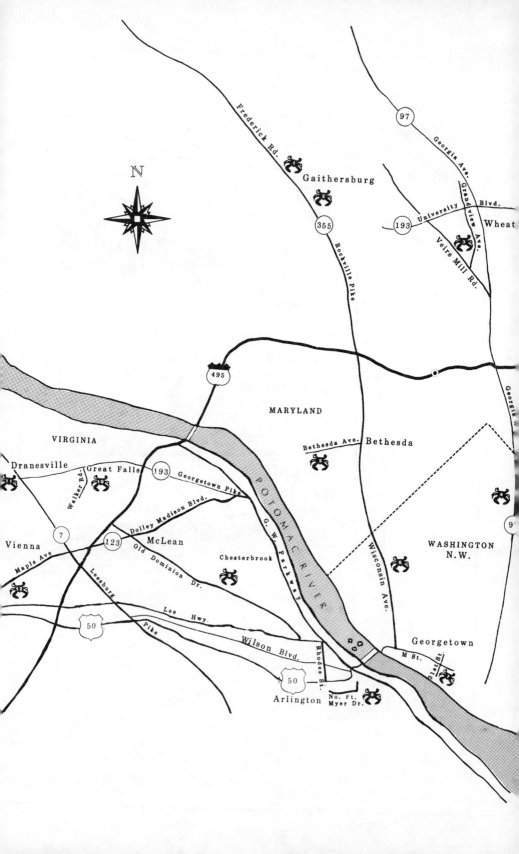

Washington
Crab Houses
NORTHWEST SECTION

1. The Cracked Claw
2. Chesapeake Crab House
3. Jim's Wheaton Crab House
4. Morgan Seafood
5. Bethesda Crab House
6. The Dancing Crab
7. Cannon Seafood
8. Quarterdeck
9. Old New Orleans Seafood Market
10. Cannon Seafood
11. C & W Seafood
12. Vienna Seafood Market

THE CRACKED CLAW

19815 Frederick Road
Gaithersburg, Maryland
301/428-0588

Business Season: year round

Hours: Tuesday through Friday—11:30 AM to 10 PM,
Saturday—5 PM to 11 PM, Sunday—5 PM to 10 PM, closed
Monday

Eat In/Carry Out

Crab Cookery: cream of crab soup and hot Louisiana and Texas
crabs

The Cracked Claw is located 2.5 miles north of the Holiday Inn. At this
country-style crab house, family groups can enjoy their crabs under a tree;
that is, under the tree that is growing in the center of the back porch, as a
unique reminder that nature and crabs go together.

Crab Casserole

1 pound crab meat	1 egg yolk, beaten
½ cup chopped celery	2 tablespoons lemon juice
2 tablespoons chopped green pepper	½ teaspoon salt
¼ cup butter	1 tablespoon butter
2 tablespoons flour	¼ cup Italian bread crumbs
1 cup milk	

Remove any shell or cartilage from crab meat. Cook celery and green
pepper in butter until tender. Blend in flour. Add milk gradually and cook
until thick, stirring constantly. Stir a little of the hot sauce into egg yolk; add
to remaining sauce, stirring constantly. Add lemon juice, seasonings, and
crab meat. Place in a well-greased 1-quart casserole. Combine butter and
crumbs; sprinkle over casserole. Bake in a moderate oven, 350° F., for 20 to
25 minutes or until brown. Serves 6.

CHESAPEAKE CRAB HOUSE
Walnut Hill Shopping Center
Route 355
Gaithersburg, Maryland
301/948-2175

Business Season: year round

Hours: Monday through Friday—11 AM to 2 PM and 5 PM to 10:30 PM, Saturday and Sunday—4 PM to 10:30 PM

Eat In/Carry Out

Crab Cookery: hot steamed crabs, crab cakes, and crab soup

Live entertainment is provided Tuesday through Sunday in the large lounge, and on Monday night, you can watch the football game. At the Chesapeake Crab House, you can "enjoy our delicious hot spiced hard shell crabs in a casual family atmosphere." Please call to reserve your jumbo crabs.

JIM'S WHEATON CRAB HOUSE
11210 Grandview Avenue
Wheaton, Maryland
301/942-CRAB

Business Season: year round

Hours: 1:30 PM to 12:30 AM

Eat In/Carry Out

Crab Cookery: crabs—hard or soft, live or steamed, and by the dozen or bushel, and she crab soup

Jim's Wheaton Crab House is a small neighborhood eatery that seats about 60 crab enthusiasts. It has earned its reputation through hard and careful work in preparing succulent hot steamed crabs time after time. At Jim's, you can enjoy your steamed crabs at small window tables which give you a view of the street, the people, and traffic, or, if you choose instead, you can view the soaps on T.V.

MORGAN SEAFOOD
3200 Georgia Avenue, N.W.
Washington, D.C.
202/829-2666

Business Season: year round

Hours: Monday through Saturday—9:30 AM to 12:30 AM, Sunday—11:30 AM to 10 PM

Carry Out Only

Crab Cookery: steamed or live hard shell crabs

Morris Morgan's Georgia Avenue location has been a hot spot since opening in 1968 on the eve of the Fourth of July. You may get a bang out of Mr. Morgan's "firecracker crabs."

BETHESDA CRAB HOUSE
4958 Bethesda Avenue
Bethesda, Maryland
301/652-9754

Business Season: year round

Hours: Monday through Saturday—9 AM to midnight,
Sunday—11 AM to midnight

Eat In/Carry Out

Crab Cookery: hot jumbo Louisiana crabs and catering
specialists for crab feasts

Henry Vechery, who has hosted crab feasts at the Bethesda Crab House
for over 20 years, recommends that reservations be made if you are planning
on a feast which is served Monday through Thursday. All you need do is
sample his delightful crabs and you may return time and time again for the
next 20 years.

THE DANCING CRAB
4611 Wisconsin Avenue, N.W.
Washington, D.C.
202/244-1882

Business Season: open all year

Hours: Monday through Saturday—11 AM to 11 PM,
Sunday—2 PM to 11 PM

Eat In/Carry Out

Crab Cookery: hot steamed crabs, crab cakes, soft shell crabs,
and crab soup

This rustic crab house with its upper Wisconsin Avenue address is
frequented by television and sports personalities. Enjoy outstanding seafood
specials every night in a relaxed atmosphere where rolled-up shirt-sleeves,
beer, and crabs are the most prominent features. "Jumbo, large, medium,
and small, we will have them ready; give us a call—please allow 30 minutes
cooking time."

CANNON SEAFOOD

Georgetown
1065 31st Street
Washington, D.C.
202/337-8366

Business Season: all year

Hours: Monday through Thursday—7:30 AM to 6 PM,
Friday—7:30 AM to 7 PM, Saturday—7:30 AM to 5:30 PM,
Sunday—closed

Carry Out Only

Crab Cookery: hard or soft crabs, live or steamed crabs, and
crab meat

Cannon Seafood traces its early beginnings to the Municipal Fish
Wharf in 1938 and to the Western Market in 1968. Today, Cannon
Seafood blends nicely with the streets of Georgetown. Bobby Moore is the
proprietor and purveyor of fresh seafoods here. He commands excellence in
all of his products and he gets it; excellent crabs are the main feature for us.

QUARTERDECK

1200 North Fort Myer Drive
Arlington, Virginia
703/528-CRAB

Business Season: all year

Hours: weekdays—6 PM to 11 PM, weekends—12 PM to 11
PM

Eat In/Carry Out

Crab Cookery: crab and spiced shrimp feast daily; J.O. Special
Blend Seasoning

The Quarterdeck, an "old hitching-post station," with a Radnor
Heights hilltop location, presents cable T.V., a wood finished bar, two
down-home sports rooms, and an outdoor patio—add outstanding steamed
crabs—need more?

226

OLD NEW ORLEANS SEAFOOD MARKET
6232 Old Dominion Drive
McLean, Virginia
703/237-7755

Business Season: all year

Hours: Monday through Friday—9 AM to 7 PM, Saturday—9 AM to 5:30 PM, closed Sundays

Carry Out Only

Crab Cookery: cajun crabs; crab meat; crab cakes; and soft, hard, live, and steamed crabs

Cajun crabs and crayfish are the specialties of Moe Cheramie. He has his crabs and crayfish prepared in New Orleans and flown in daily to his old New Orleans style seafood market. It is located in the Chesterbrook Shopping Center.

The following is Moe's recipe for Louisiana Fried Hard crabs.

Louisiana Fried Hard Crabs

8 large hard raw crabs, cleaned

fats and eggs, season with salt and pepper

4 cups oil

salt and pepper

¼ cup oil plus 3 tbs.

Rinse fats and eggs, pour off water. Remove top shell, apron, claws, legs and gills from crabs. Remove fat and egg from shells. Reserve. Add 4 cups oil or enough to cover crabs. Season crabs to taste. Fry in hot oil 5 minutes on the side, then turn and fry 5 minutes more. In small pot on low, cook fat and egg in remaining oil for 20 minutes. Serve egg mixture over rice. This recipe may be easily doubled.

CANNON SEAFOOD
762A Walker Road
Great Falls, Virginia
703/759-4950

Business Season: all year

Hours: Tuesday through Friday—10 AM to 7 PM, Saturday—9 AM to 6 PM, Sunday and Monday—closed

Carry Out Only

Crab Cookery: caters to crab feasts and specializes in bushel sales of crabs—hard or soft, live or steamed

Crabs, as we all know, have suddenly become something this nation of meat eaters cannot do without. Since Cannon Seafood is frequented by discriminating crab lovers who expect the best and get it, you should take the clue and add this stop to your next crab eating adventure.

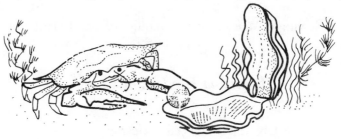

C & W SEAFOOD
11521 Leesburg Pike
Dranesville, Virginia
703/450-4472

Business Season: open year round—crabs in summer

Hours: 10 AM to 7 PM

Carry Out Only

Crab Cookery: hot steamed crabs, oysters, and live crabs

This roadside seafood market is located halfway between Tyson's Corner and Leesburg, Virginia. It offers easy access to Bay delights for travelers using the busy Route 7 corridor. Baltimore Spice Seafood Seasoning and fat crabs are your reason for trying C & W's tasty crabs.

VIENNA SEAFOOD MARKET

328 Maple Avenue, West
Vienna, Virginia
703/938-0736

Business Season: open all year

Hours: Monday through Thursday—8 AM to 7 PM, Friday—
8 AM to 8 PM, Saturday—10 AM to 8 PM, Sunday—1 PM to
6 PM

Carry Out Only

Crab Cookery: hard crabs—live or steamed

Richard Moss opened his Vienna Seafood Market in September 1974
and has, over the last 10 years, built a tremendous following for his delicious
steamed crabs. We returned recently and our crabs were cooked just right.
The jumbo Texas crabs are the house special and rate the highest marks.

Broiled Crab Meat in Shells

1 pound crab meat

⅓ cup butter

2 tablespoons lemon juice

¼ teaspoon salt

Dash cayenne pepper

Chopped parsley

Chopped thyme

Remove any shell or cartilage from crab meat. Combine butter, lemon
juice, salt, cayenne pepper, and crab meat. Place in 6 well-greased,
individual shells or 5-ounce custard cups. Place on a broiler pan about 4
inches from source of heat. Broil for 7 to 10 minutes or until brown. Garnish
with parsley and thyme, sprinkled over top of each shell. Serves 6.

Hard shells, watermelons, and much, much
more—you will find them all at Johnson's Store.

Johnson's Store illustration is adapted from photograph by Craig Herndon, Washington Post.

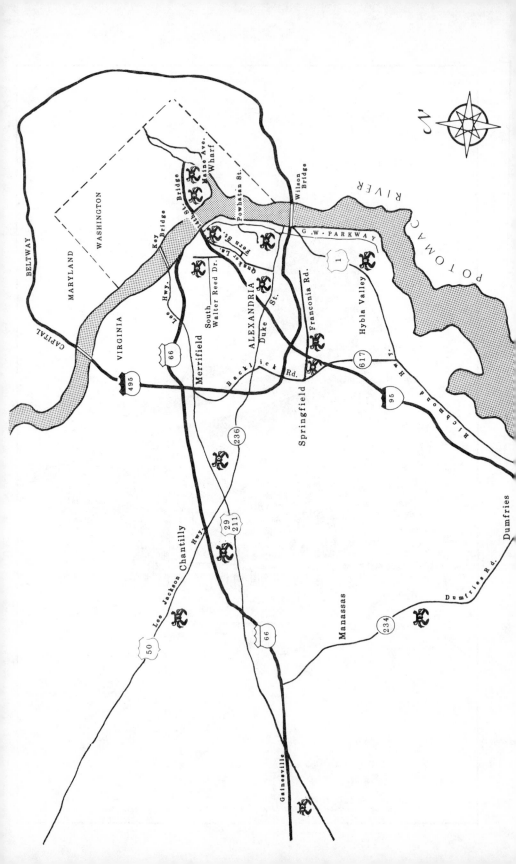

Washington
Crab Houses
SOUTHWEST SECTION

1. Municipal Fish Wharf
2. Morgan Seafood
3. Captain Mike's Seafood
4. Ernie's Original Crab House
5. Johnson's Store
6. Bobby's Great American Crab House
7. House of Crabs
8. Ernie's Original Crab House
9. Vienna Seafood Market
10. Fairfax Crab House
11. Sam's Crab House
12. Blue Ridge Seafood
13. Crosby Crab Co.
14. Janet's Place

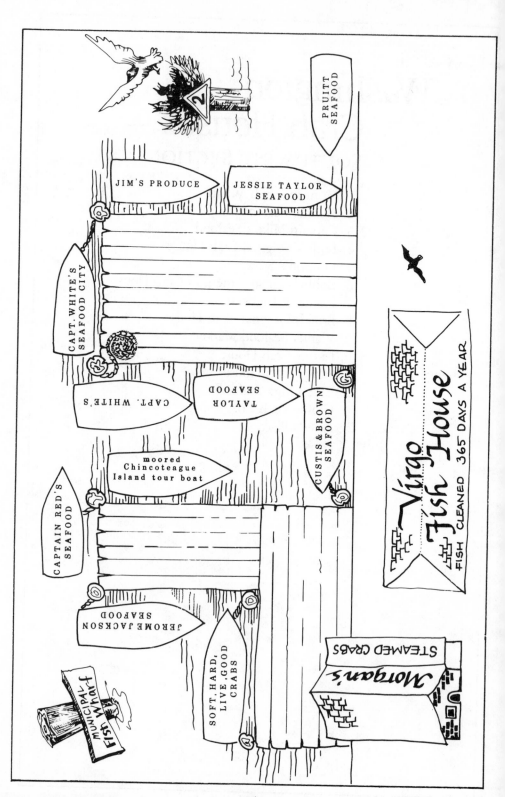

MUNICIPAL FISH WHARF
1100 Maine Avenue, S.W.
Washington, D.C.

Business Season: all year

Hours: 9 AM to 9 PM, 7 days

Carry Out Only

Dockage Available: Washington Channel, Potomac River

Crab Cookery: live crabs, hard crabs, soft crabs, steamed crabs, crab meat, and all boats specialize in bushel sales

Custis and Brown Seafood
202/484-0168
Boat—"Cathy C"

Capt. White's Seafood City
202/554-5520
Boat—"Sue Constance"

Jerome Jackson Seafood
202/484-3820
Boat—"Wayne Christy"

Captain Red's Seafood
202/554-5170
Boat—"Miss Maxine"

Pruitt Seafood
202/554-2669
Boat—"Ruth & Annie" and "Wanda"

Jessie Taylor Seafood
202/554-4173
Boat—"Jessie"

235

MORGAN SEAFOOD

(at the wharf)
Washington Channel, Potomac River
202/488-8145

Business Season: year round

Hours: 9 AM to 10 PM, 7 days a week

Carry Out Only

Dockage Available: Washington Channel

Crab Cookery: hot steamed or live crabs

Morgan's is the only merchant to offer hot steamed crabs at the waterfront. It is located on the roadside at the municipal fish wharf and, since it is actually on dry land, it has the steaming pots and equipment to prepare delicious steamed crabs.

CAPTAIN MIKE'S SEAFOOD

1621 South Walter Reed Drive
Arlington, Virginia
703/486-2250

Business Season: all year

Hours: 10 AM to 10 PM, 7 days

Carry Out Only

Crab Cookery: hot steamed crabs, live crabs, and crab meat

Captain Mike Kelly specializes in hot steamed crabs. They are steamed to perfection while you wait, eager and ready to taste this delicious gift from the Bay.

ERNIE'S ORIGINAL CRAB HOUSE
1623 Fern Street
Alexandria, Virginia
703/836-1623 or 836-1624

Business Season: March 1st to December 15th

Hours: noon to 11 PM, 7 days a week

Eat In/Carry Out

Crab Cookery: hot steamed crabs

This Ernie's location is owned and operated by the Pak family, who takes great pride in the service and preparation of delicious steamed crabs. Stop by the crab feast any time from 5 PM to 10 PM daily.

JOHNSON'S STORE
1413 Powhatan Street
Alexandria, Virginia
703/548-6888

Business Season: March to December

Hours: 8 AM to 8 PM daily

Carry Out Only

Crab Cookery: steamed hard shell crabs, deviled crabs, and crab cakes

Hard shells, watermelons, and much, much more—you will find them all at Johnson's Store. Crabs sold here are prepared in Colonial Beach, Virginia and trucked in daily.

BOBBY'S GREAT AMERICAN CRAB HOUSE
4231 Duke Street
Alexandria, Virginia
703/823-5111

Business Season: all year

Hours: Monday through Friday—11:30 AM to 10 PM, Saturday and Sunday—1 PM to 11 PM

Eat In/Carry Out

Crab Cookery: crab cakes, soft crab sandwich, hot crab 'n' cheese on a croissant roll, and hot steamed crabs.

Bobby Gerber welcomes you to his Great American Crab House with the following:

"It is my policy to provide you with the very best crabs available. Due to the season, Mother Nature, and the geographical source, the quality of crabs varies. Please don't hesitate to ask for a replacement if you are not satisfied with your crab. Now. . .enjoy yourself and thank you for your patronage."

HOUSE OF CRABS
6141 Franconia Road
Alexandria, Virginia
703/922-9832

Business Season: all year

Hours: Monday through Friday—11:30 AM to 11 PM, Saturday and Sunday—2 PM to 11 PM

Eat In/Carry Out

Crab Cookery: crab vegetable soup, crab cakes, and hot steamed crabs

Crabs, of course, are a happy answer to the current preoccupation with health and fitness, and they are always a rewarding dish. At the House of Crabs, you can enjoy your tasty crabs in a seaworthy atmosphere. The cozy dining room has portholes, wooden pulleys, riggings, maps of waterways, fishnets, anchors, and ropes, which all contribute to an enjoyable experience of eating crabs.

ERNIE'S ORIGINAL CRAB HOUSE
7929 Richmond Highway
Alexandria, Virginia
703/780-0100

Business Season: all year; closed during bad weather

Hours: Monday through Friday—6 PM to 10 PM, Saturday and Sunday—noon to 10 PM

Eat In/Carry Out

Crab Cookery: hot steamed crabs and crab cakes

The original owner of this highly successful crab house chain was Ernie DelVecchio, who was a pioneer in the crab business. Ernie was one of the first men in the area to import crabs from Louisiana and extend his operation to a year round crab business. Today, this restaurant is owned by Joe Jarboe who worked for Ernie for 7 years prior to taking over in 1975. Joe is a proud and capable crab cooker and welcomes you to his crab feast held 7 days a week. Please call for details.

VIENNA SEAFOOD MARKET
6681-29 Backlick Road
Springfield, Virginia
703/569-2722

Business Season: all year

Hours: Monday through Saturday—10 AM to 8 PM, closed Sunday

Carry Out Only

Crab Cookery: crab meat, hard crabs, soft crabs, and hot steamed crabs

Vienna Seafood Market of Springfield is located in the Backlick Shopping Center and is a seafood market catering to fresh seafood delicacies.

FAIRFAX CRAB HOUSE
8815 Lee Highway
Fairfax, Virginia
703/560-0060

Business Season: year round

Hours: weekdays—3 PM to midnight; Friday, Saturday, and Sunday—2 PM to midnight

Eat In/Carry Out

Crab Cookery: crab feast available and hot steamed crabs

Capt. Pell's Fairfax Crab House is located on Lee Highway between the rolling hills of Merrifield and Fairfax, Virginia.

When you order crabs at Fairfax Crab House, they are piled high on a spread of butcher paper and are ready to be pulled apart by human fingers, paring knife, or a wooden mallet. As you are being served, make a note of the cartoons featuring the blue crab. This art is the work of the waitresses who serve you. That should tell you something about their dedication to your crab eating experience.

SAM'S CRAB HOUSE
13623 Lee Jackson Highway
Dart Chantilly Mall
Chantilly, Virginia
703/378-6177

Business Season: all year

Hours: Monday through Saturday—11 AM to 11 PM, Sunday—12 PM to 10 PM

Eat In/Carry Out

Crab Cookery: she crab soup, crab cakes, and daily crab feast (Monday through Friday—5 PM to 11 PM, Saturday and Sunday—2 PM to 11 PM)

Sam's special, hot steamed crabs come in small, medium, large, or jumbo sizes. They are served by the dozen. Since prices may vary with the supply and the season, check with your waitress for the going rate.

Sam's special recipe for crab cakes is made from a delicate combination of crab meat, cracker meal, celery, carrots, onions, mustard, mayonnaise, wine, and worcestershire sauce. Sound's good, doesn't it?

240

BLUE RIDGE SEAFOOD
15704 Lee Highway
Gainesville, Virginia
703/754-9852

Business Season: March to December

Hours: Monday through Thursday—3 PM to 10 PM; Friday, Saturday, and Sunday—3 PM to 11 PM

Eat In/Carry Out

Crab Cookery: Blue Crabs, Blue Ribbon, and Blue Ridge

Blue Ridge Seafood was known as the Blue Ridge Farm Restaurant for 22 years before Rod and Cora took over in July 1979. Since that time, they have spread the word of good crab cooking from the foothills to the city.

CROSBY CRAB CO.
14718 Dumfries Road
Manassas, Virginia
703/791-5804

Business Season: all year

Hours: Monday through Thursday—11 AM to 7 PM, Friday and Saturday—11 AM to 8 PM, Sunday—1 PM to 7:30 PM

Carry Out Only

Crab Cookery: hard or soft crabs, live or steamed crabs, J.O. Spice

This "old gas station" of the 1930's is now home to a country roadside crab market. Andy and Carolyn Crosby specialize in daily bushel sales. A wide range of shellfish is available to choose from. The service is friendly, efficient, and prompt.

JANET'S PLACE
12208 Lee Highway
Fairfax, Virginia
703/830-1265

Business Season: all year

Hours: Monday through Wednesday—10:30 AM to 9:30 PM, Thursday through Sunday—10:30 AM to 11:00 PM

Eat In/Carry Out

Crab Cookery: hot steamed crabs, crab cakes, and soft shell crabs

Janet Robinson is the owner, crab cooker, bartender and Bar-B-Q maker at her delightful roadside spot that is worthy of a stop. Her delicious specialties include North Carolina jumbo chopped BBQ, Idaho french fries, Ohio hot dogs with chili, New York steak subs and our favorite, of course, Maryland and Virginia steamed crabs. Simply delicious!

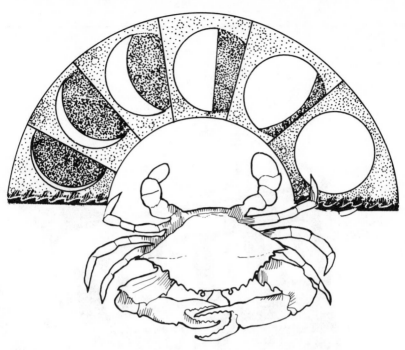

Experts say that:

"The greatest amount of shedding takes place during the summer in the early morning hours, a week before the full moon, or one hour after the high tide."

"Watermen say that hard crabs have more meat in them when the moon is on the wane, & that soft crabs are best and most plentiful when the moon is full..."

from "Call It Delmarvalous"
"Chesapeake Kaleidoscope"

The Baltimore Spice Company

Ralph Brunn, Executive Vice President of The Baltimore Spice Company, and his father, Gustav, are directly responsible for the creation of OLD BAY seasoning. The bustling Baltimore waterfront of 1939 found Gustav's new spice business on the second floor of a building located across from Baltimore's fish market.

Today, The Baltimore Spice Company is the world's largest spice company with plants extended to major cities around the world. Traditionally, Baltimore Spice prepares individual and highly secret crab seasonings for crab houses around the Chesapeake Bay. Every order is a special one. All a crab house has to do is contact the Baltimore Spice Company and order its particular blend. The order is then prepared with care using the best quality ingredients and precise proportioning. Some crab houses have been on record for many years.

OLD BAY Seafood Seasoning is The Baltimore Spice Company's only retail product and is the country's best selling seafood seasoning.

OLD BAY is a mixture of celery, salt, pepper, mustard, pimiento, cloves, laurel leaves, mace, cardamon, ginger, cassia, and paprika—the exact blend is a Brunn family secret handed down from father to son!

While OLD BAY is known primarily for seasoning crabs and shrimp, it can also be a tasty addition when used in other foods. OLD BAY adds a lively flavor when sprinkled in soups and salads and it can turn Bloody Mary beautiful. It's perfect for poultry, hamburger, and other meats , and it is truly a versatile, all-purpose seasoning.

Hot Steamed Crabs

"If they ain't kickin', they ain't cookin'."

"Cooked to order"

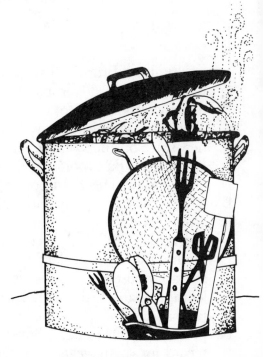

Small
Medium
Large
Jumbo
by the dozen—by the bushel

The price one would expect to pay for a dozen crabs or a bushel of crabs will vary according to season, size and where the crab is from.

The crab house's aim is to provide you with the finest available Chesapeake Bay blue crabs, supplemented by other markets when local supplies diminish. The prime crab season is April to November. From November to April, the crab merchants expand their source of crabs to the entire Atlantic seaboard and the Gulf of Mexico. In some cases, crabs are flown in from Texas and Louisiana.

There are times when the medium size crabs are running relatively heavier than the large, that is, the smaller crab is more solidly filled and is a better buy. But, for the most part, the bigger the crab, the bigger the price.

Every crab house and crab market has its method of culling crabs, but ask to see the crabs and then judge for yourself the size and quality to suit your needs.

Live Hard Crabs

LOCAL, FAT N' HEAVY HARD SHELL CRABS

Clean, green crabs are the key to buying live hard crabs. Although more olive drab in color, the "blue crab" or "blue channel" derives its name from the brilliant coloration of its large pincher claws.

When purchasing live blue crabs, buy only crabs that are alive and kicking.

To be a "keeper," the male must measure 5 inches tip to tip; females must measure 3 ½ inches. The price of the female is usually lower than the price of the male because the males grow larger and bring more market value while most females are sent to the picking houses. Blue crabs are graded and sold by the dozen or by the bushel.

Classification:	Common Name:
#1 large males	"Jimmies" or "Selects"
#2 medium males	"Mediums"
#3 fat females	"Sooks"

Soft Shell Crabs

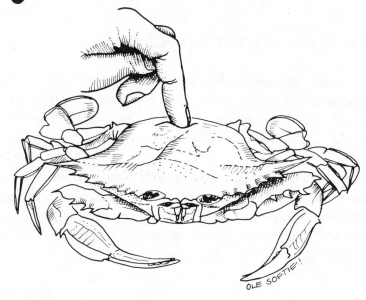

OLE SOFTIE!

LIVE, FRESH DRESSED OR FROZEN

In order for a blue crab to increase in size, the crab must first shed its hard shell, under which is a new, soft shell. The delectable "soft shell crab" must be caught right after it has molted. If left in the water, its shell will begin to harden in about two hours.

Soft shell crabs are produced from late spring to early fall with May through August the most productive months. As the availability of crabs increases, prices will drop. Some methods for preparing soft shells are baked, sautéed, deep fat fried or pan fried. Other ways of cooking will give equally tasty results. Soft shell crab sandwiches are one of life's greatest pleasures.

Soft crabs are marketed in the following manner:

Medium	2.5 to 4.0 inches
Hotel	4.0 to 4.5 inches
Prime	4.5 to 5.0 inches
Jumbo	5.0 to 5.5 inches
Whale	over 5.5 inches

Crab Meat

FRESH, HAND-PICKED CRAB MEAT

When you buy fresh-picked crab meat, it is important to realize the differences in the types of meat. Crab meat is typically packaged in one pound plastic containers. It will yield two to three cups of meat and will serve four to six persons adequately.

The five most commonly used types of crab meat are as follows:

Backfin or Lump Meat: solid lumps of white meat picked from the backfin section. Lump meat is more expensive than other packs (the top of the line).

Special: meat from the body portion of the crab and will include some lump meat.

Regular: small pieces of white meat from the body.

Claw Meat: meat picked from the claws of the crab; meat is of a darker tint, is less expensive than other grades but tastes as good.

Cocktail Claw: the claw of the crab is left partially intact leaving the meat exposed and is served as an appetizer.

ALSO RECOMMENDED

The following listing of crab merchants will be expanded in our next edition. Meanwhile, be sure to include them on your crab-eating list.

CORKY'S INC.
 SEAFOOD MARKET
Rt. 301
La Plata, Maryland
301-932-0841 301-932-1647

DANDY CRABS
10915 Baltimore Avenue
Beltsville, Maryland
301-937-2505

FIN & CLAW SEAFOOD MARKET
Smallwood Village Center
St. Charles/Waldorf, Maryland
301-645-3373
301-645-CLAW

KENT ISLAND SEAFOOD
1326 Belair Road
Bel Air, Maryland
301-877-9768

MACHO CRABS SEAFOOD, INC.
Baltimore Boulevard
Beltsville, Maryland
301-937-3615

MARYLAND WHOLESALE
 SEAFOOD MARKET
7901 Oceano Avenue
Jessup, Maryland
301-799-0141

MOE'S ROLLING CRABS
Highway 210
Oxon Hill, Maryland

PRODUCE FARM MARKET
Tyler Avenue & Forest Drive
Annapolis, Maryland
301-269-5380

SANDGATES INN
Sandgate Road
Mechanicsville, MD
301-373-5100

SEA CATCH
655 Deale Road
Deale, Maryland
301-867-3260

U.S. FISH INC.
1108 Oronoco Street
Alexandria, Virginia
703-684-0090

WOODBINE INN
Rt. 94
Woodbine, Maryland
301-442-2399

CRAB COOKERY TERMS

BACKFIN CRAB CAKES: 100-percent backfin crab meat is used to prepare these crab cakes; no filler is added.

CRAB CATERING: Steamed crabs are made readily available to the crab lover in his own back yard. In some cases the crab house can supply 24 bushels in 25 minutes—hot on the spot.

COCKTAIL CLAWS: The claw of the crab is left partially intact, leaving the meat exposed. It is served as an appetizer; it goes well with a dip of hot mustard or ketchup and horseradish.

CRAB AU GRATIN: Crab lumps are sautéed in butter sauce.

CRAB CAKE: A delicate combination of crab meat, cracker meal, crackers, onion, mustard, mayonnaise and worcestershire sauce is fried to a golden brown. This recipe can be enhanced by using more crab meat and less filler.

CRAB FEAST: Usually means all the crabs you can eat for a set price and, in some cases, a time limit is set. Please inquire for details.

CRAB FLUFF: This is a stuffed crab that is dipped in a house batter and fried to a golden brown.

CRAB NEWBURG: Crab lumps are cooked in cheese sauce.

CRAB NORFOLK: Crab lumps are sautéed in butter and wine.

CRAB SOUP, CREAM OF: This is a thicker, hardier soup made by simmering crab in seasoned milk or cream.

CRAB SOUP, VEGETABLE STYLE: This soup will probably be a little different each time it is prepared depending on the vegetables you use. The ingredients can be amended to suit your taste using whatever items you have on hand.

DEVILED CRAB: Save the top shell of a cooked crab. Pick the crab meat and make into your favorite crab cake. Stuff the cake into the shell and then bake. You can top with ¼ slice of bacon and then grill until done.

FRIED HARD CRAB: A cooked crab is cleaned and stuffed with crab meat, then quick-fried to a golden brown.

IMPERIAL CRAB: Named after Queen Henrietta Marie, imperial crab is a savory blend of backfin crab meat, mayonnaise, and seasonings. Only the best ingredients are used here.

LIVE CRABS: Live crabs are made available for the crab lover to cook at home.

SHE CRAB SOUP: She crab soup is a cream soup to which the crab meat and roe are added with seasonings to taste—salt, pepper, worcestershire sauce, a dash of sherry and a sprinkle of fresh herbs.

SOFT CRAB SANDWICH: Soft shell crab is quick fried and placed between two slices of bread. This is one of life's delights. Close your eyes and let your taste buds savor.

STEAMED CRAB: Freshly caught blue crab pulled from the water and popped in the pot is steamed with Old Bay Seasoning or J.O. Seasoning for 20 minutes.

ACKNOWLEDGEMENTS

Tab Tire Repair, Upper Marlboro, Maryland
Falls Camera, Arlington, Virginia
Curry Copy, Alexandria, Virginia
Pica & Points Typography, Alexandria, Virginia
St. Mary's Press, Hollywood, Maryland
Antietam Pottery, Keedysville, Maryland

Dean Gore   Gabe Fleri
Dave Silver   Jay Freschi
Kenny Kans   Jane Sita
Laura Majorana   Dana Austin Lawhorne

EDITORS

Lynne Haas   Linda Brudvig

Annie Hendricks   Van Ochs

ALPHABETICAL CRAB HOUSE LISTING

ALPHABETICAL CRAB HOUSE LISTING

ALPHABETICAL CRAB HOUSE LISTING

ALPHABETICAL CRAB HOUSE LISTING

EDITOR'S NOTE

Our intent has been to make this volume the total resource book on the Chesapeake Bay Blue Crab. We have attempted to include every important attraction that the crab lover may encounter. As in all types of businesses, there are openings and closings. We welcome any new openings and request that you inform us if your favorite crab eatery is not listed. Since compiling our listing, the following establishments are no longer in operation.

Chesapeake Crab House
Gaithersburg, Maryland

Newton Seafood
Fredericksburg, Virginia

Blue Seas Crab House
Reisterstown, Maryland

Mel's Crab House
Owings Mills, Maryland

Mug and Mallet
Salisbury, Maryland

The Crab Shack
Baltimore, Maryland

J. A. Jacobs Seafoods
Rockhall, Maryland

King Crab Co.
Hampton, Virginia

Capt. Jim's Seafood Kettle
Queenstown, Maryland

Captain Kidd's
Restaurant and Marina
Virginia Beach, Virginia

Tappahannock Seafood
Tappahannock, Virginia

Newton Seafood
Fredericksburg, Virginia

Chesapeake Crab House
Gaithersburg, Maryland

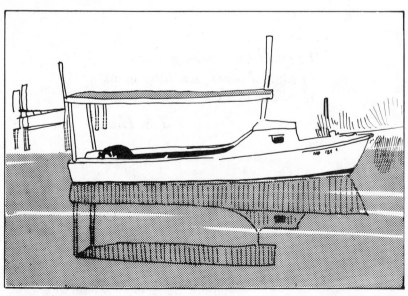

I should have been a pair
of ragged claws, scuttling across
the floor of silent seas.

T.S. Eliot

Whitey Schmidt, author and publisher of *The Official Crab Eater's Guide,* was born on the banks of the Potomac River. Over 35 years ago, his father, Pop Schmidt, gave Whitey his first hot steamed crab at the Old Midway Tavern, a local neighborhood eatery. Since that first crab eating experience, Whitey has spent a lifetime searching out the best steamed crabs. He has combined personal interest and knowledge of the local areas and has spent the last 4 years criss-crossing the back-bay regions researching the Blue Crab. Whitey continues his pursuit of the delectable and elusive Blue Crab that has resulted in *The Official Crab Eater's Guide* and is hard at work on several bay related books.

Author's illustration is adapted from photograph by Linda S. Brudvig.

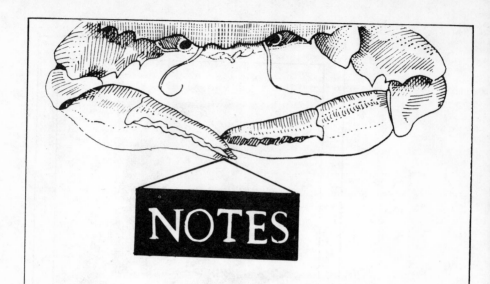

NOTES